MAKE 'EM LAUGH & TAKE THEIR MONEY

Dan S. Kennedy

GLAZER-KENNEDY PUBLISHING

Copyright © 2010 Dan Kennedy

ISBN: 978-0-98237-934-9
Library of Congress Control Number: 2009941944

Published by:
GLAZER-KENNEDY PUBLISHING
An Imprint of Morgan James Publishing, LLC
1225 Franklin Ave Ste 32
Garden City, NY 11530-1693
Toll Free 800-485-4943
www.MorganJamesPublishing.com

Cover/Interior Design by:
Rachel Lopez
rachel@r2cdesign.com

In an effort to support local communities, raise awareness and funds, Morgan James Publishing donates one percent of all book sales for the life of each book to Habitat for Humanity. Get involved today, visit **www.HelpHabitatForHumanity.org.**

The Most Incredible
FREE Gift Ever

($613.91 Worth of Pure Money-Making Information)

Dan Kennedy & Bill Glazer are offering an incredible opportunity for you to see WHY Glazer-Kennedy Insider's Circle™ is known as "THE PLACE" where entrepreneurs seeking FAST and Dramatic Growth and greater Control, Independence, and Security come together, Dan & Bill want to give you **$613.91 worth of pure Money-Making Information** including TWO months as an 'Elite' Gold Member of Glazer-Kennedy's Insider's Circle™. You'll receive a steady stream of MILLIONAIRE Maker Information including:

* Glazer-Kennedy University: Series of 3 Webinars (Value = $387.00)

The 10 "BIG Breakthroughs in Business Life *with Dan Kennedy*
- HOW <u>Any</u> Entrepreneur or Sales Professional can Multiply INCOME by 10X
- **HOW to Avoid Once and for All being an *"Advertising Victim"***
- The *"Hidden Goldmine"* in Everyone's Business and HOW to Capitalize on it
- **The BIGGEST MISTAKE most Entrepreneurs make in their Marketing**
- And the BIGGEEE...Getting Customers Seeking You Out.

The ESSENTIALS to Writing Million Dollar Ads & Sales Letters BOTH
Online & Offline *with Marketing & Advertising Coach, Bill Glazer*
- How to INCREASE the Selling Power of <u>All</u> Your Advertising by Learning the 13 "Must Have" Direct Response Principles
- **Key Elements that Determine the Success of Your Website**
- HOW to Craft a Headline the Grabs the Reader's Attention
- **How to Create an Irresistible Offer that Melts Away <u>Any</u> Resistance to Buy**
- The <u>Best</u> Ways to Create Urgency and Inspire IMMEDIATE Response
- *"Insider Strategies"* to INCREASE Response that you <u>Must</u> be using both **ONLINE & Offline**

The ESSENTIALS of Productivity & Implementation for Entrepreneurs *w/*
Peak Performance Coach Lee Milteer
- How to Almost INSTANTLY be MORE Effective, Creative, Profitable, and Take MORE Time Off
- **HOW to Master the "Inner Game" of Personal Peak Productivity**
- How to Get MORE Done in Less Time
- **HOW to Get Others to Work On <u>Your</u> Schedule**
- How to Create Clear Goals for SUCCESSFUL Implementation
- And Finally the BIGGEE...How to Stop Talking and Planning Your Dreams and Start Implementing Them into Reality

* 'Elite' Gold Insider's Circle Membership (Two Month Value = $99.94):

- Two Issues of *The No B.S.® Marketing Letter:*

  Each issue is at least 12 pages – usually MORE – Overflowing with **the latest Marketing & MoneyMaking Strategies**. Current members refer to it as a day-long intense seminar in print, arriving by first class mail every month. There are ALWAYS terrific examples of *"What's-Working-NOW"* **Strategies**, timely Marketing news, trends, ongoing teaching of Dan Kennedy's Most IMPORTANT Strategies... and MORE. As soon as it arrives in your mailbox you'll want to find a quiet place, grab a highlighter, and devour every word.

IV BONUS

- Two CDs Of The **EXCLUSIVE GOLD AUDIO INTERVIEWS**

  These are EXCLUSIVE interviews with successful users of direct response advertising, leading experts and entrepreneurs in direct marketing, and famous business authors and speakers. Use them to turn commuting hours into "POWER Thinking" hours.

  ### * The New Member No B.S.® Income Explosion Guide & CD (Value = $29.97)
  This resource is especially designed for NEW MEMBERS to show them HOW they can join the thousands of Established Members **creating exciting sales and PROFIT growth** in their Business, Practices, or Sales Careers & Greater SUCCESS in their Business lives.

  ### Income Explosion FAST START Tele-Seminar with Dan Kennedy, Bill Glazer, and Lee Milteer (Value = $97.00)
  Attend from the privacy and comfort of your home or office…hear a DYNAMIC discussion of Key Advertising, Marketing, Promotion, Entrepreneurial & Phenomenon strategies, PLUS answers to the most Frequently Asked Questions about these Strategies

* You'll also get these Exclusive "Members Only" Perks:

- **Special FREE Gold Member CALL-IN TIMES:** Several times a year, Dan & I schedule Gold-Member ONLY Call-In times
- **Gold Member RESTRICTED ACCESS WEBSITE:** Past issues of the *No B.S.® Marketing Letter*, articles, special news, etc.
- **Continually Updated MILLION DOLLAR RESOURCE DIRECTORY** with Contacts and Resources Dan & his clients use.

To activate your MOST INCREDIBLE FREE GIFT EVER you only pay a one-time charge of $19.95 (or $39.95 for Int'l subscribers) to cover postage (this is for everything). **After your 2-Month FREE test-drive, you will automatically continue at the lowest Gold Member price of $59.97 per month. Should you decide to cancel your membership, you can do so at any time by calling Glazer-Kennedy Insider's Circle™ at 410-825-8600 or faxing a cancellation note to 410-825-3301 (Monday through Friday 9am – 5pm). Remember, your credit card will NOT be charged the low monthly membership fee until the beginning of the 3rd month, which means you will receive 2 full issues to read, test, and profit from all of the powerful techniques and strategies you get from being an Insider's Circle Gold Member. And of course, it's impossible for you to lose, because if you don't absolutely LOVE everything you get, you can simply cancel your membership before the third month and never get billed a single penny for membership.**

---

*EMAIL REQUIRED IN ORDER TO NOTIFY YOU ABOUT THE
GLAZER-KENNEDY UNIVERSITY WEBINARS AND FAST START TELESEMINAR*

Name _____ Business Name _____

Address _____

City _____ State _____ Zip _____ e-mail* _____

Phone _____ Fax _____

Credit Card Instructions to Cover $19.95 for Shipping & Handling:

_____Visa _____MasterCard _____ American Express _____ Discover

Credit Card Number _____ Exp. Date _____

Signature _____ Date _____

Providing this information constitutes your permission for Glazer-Kennedy Insider's Circle™ to contact you regarding related information via mail, e-mail, fax, and phone.

FAX BACK TO 410-825-3301
Or mail to: 401 Jefferson Ave, Towson, MD 21286

DEDICATED TO
DR. HERB TRUE

There are many people who've helped me with understanding and using humor. But Herb deserves special recognition. His a gentle, compassionate comedy without a milligram of meanness in it, on which he built a very successful speaking career, a teaching legacy at Notre Dame, and took on saintly missions like teaching self-esteem to people at homeless shelters. A far better, more generous man and citizen than I. One of Herb's books was appropriately titled 'Humor Power' – through humor, he has been a powerful influence on countless thousands of people. And a source of great material for hundreds of thieving speakers and writers, me included. I'd apologize, but I have Conscience Deficiency Syndrome.

Humor may have greater power than any other aspect of communication: to tear down and destroy, to compel thought, to encourage compassion, to persuade, to motivate, to ease pain, to affect the outcome of an election and the future of a nation or to make an evening with friends a great memory, or even to sustain a friendship over time. And, of course, to sell things, which is what I have been using it for, making my living, for more than 30 years. Herb would be very pleased if you used your own humor to sell another set of pots and pans or insurance policy or automobile or time-share, but even more pleased if you used it to save a soul or help some grieving person recover or some other higher purpose. I will be pleased if you find some parts of this book funny, and the book helps you to be funnier for any purpose – any less serious, sourpuss minutes is a plus. But whether that happens or not, I'm pleased you bought the book. There's a reason they collect the cover charge at the comedy club when you go in, not on your way out.

> *"A nice little old lady cashed a check at the supermarket and thanked the manager profusely. 'I just don't know what I'd do without people like you now that the bank has stopped cashing my checks.'"*
>
> *- Herb True*

ABOUT THE AUTHOR

DAN **K**ENNEDY is the author of 13 business books – all, miraculously, in print and on bookstore shelves simultaneously, the oldest first published in 1991, a circus feat of longevity. His books are loaded with humor, whether you see anything funny in them or not. A couple even include cartoons. Rich Karlgaard, editor at *Forbes*, favorably compared Dan's writing style to famed novelist Thomas Wolfe's. (*Bonfire of the Vanities*). Dan's own editor at one of his publishers very unfavorably compared his writing style to a drunken chimpanzee left alone with a typewriter everyday in the asylum, after his electro-shock treatments. The fact that Dan makes more money in a year from writing than she makes from her craft in a decade has not influenced her opinion. Dan's books have earned spots on *Inc. Magazine*'s 100 Best Business Books List, *Business Week* bestseller list, and Amazon's bestseller lists. They have been translated in 8 different languages and published in over 14 different countries. None have been an Oprah Book Club selection.

He also writes seven business newsletters every month; a weekly fax; at gunpoint, a blog ; and a series of articles syndicated to more than 200 different industry and professional newsletters.

He is also a political columnist/satirist, with a weekly column appearing most weeks at BusinessAndMedia.org, affiliated with the Media Research Center in Washington D.C.

As a speaker, Dan's 30 year career includes 9-1/2 consecutive years on the #1 public seminar tour in America addressing audiences of 10,000 to 35,000, and sharing the platform not only with the great success philosophers of our day – Zig Ziglar, Brian Tracy, Jim Rohn – but with former U.S. Presidents (one of whom was funny), other world leaders and political figures, top corporate CEO's and entrepreneurs, pro athletes, and countless Hollywood celebrities, including comedian Bill Cosby and broadcasting legend Larry King. Also, at Glazer-Kennedy Insider's Circle™ events, he has appeared with Ivanka Trump, George Foreman, Joan Rivers and even Gene Simmons – making Dan an opening act for KISS. Dan has also appeared on programs with Donald Trump, who is funny, and with Tony Robbins, who is unintentionally, screamingly funny. Dan has performed repeatedly in more than 35 major sports arenas, the showroom at the Stardust in Las Vegas, on a cruise ship, a flooded parking lot during a hurricane in Key West, and in more Holiday Inn meeting rooms smelling of cheap disinfectant and burnt coffee than he cares to count. In 25 years of membership in the National Speakers Association, as one of its most successful and celebrated members, he received no awards, was never invited to speak at a convention general session, was tossed out once and had to sue to get reinstated and won, and always attended association meetings accompanied by a food taster – and he isn't the least bit bitter about any of it.

Over 1,000 peers; other professional speakers have attended Dan's specialized business training seminars for that industry, invested in his home study courses about the speaking business, and/or retained him for private consulting. Many will admit it.

Dan is also on the Advisory Board of the School of Communications at High Point University. (HPU.com). Go figure.

Dan lives with his second and third wives and their Million Dollar Dog in Ohio and Virginia. His office is in Phoenix.

He is actively engaged in the very funny sport of harness racing, which has nearly gotten him killed on three occasions.

Information about Dan's other books can be accessed at nobsbooks. com and DanKennedy.com

Favorable comments about this book may be sent directly to the author at Fax# 602-269-3113 or c/o Kennedy Inner Circle Inc., 5818 N. 7th Street #103, Phoenix, AZ 85014, and will be responded to. Bomb threats have long ago become too commonplace and are ignored. Inquiries about having Dan speak to your group (should you have a death wish), be a guest on your tele-seminar, write for your publication, or otherwise do something you are willing to pay for should be directed to this office. Letters arriving with $100.00 bills attached move to the front of the line. Extremely attractive, busty women should not send nude photos instead of the money. He's married, he's old, and, frankly, it's become so routine and frequent, it's mundane.

The business organization developed around Dan, *Glazer-Kennedy Insider's Circle*™, connects with over 250,000 entrepreneurs, business owners and sales and marketing professionals weekly via online media, influences millions annually, has over 25,000 dues-paying Members (a few of which are deceased and still paying) at four different membership levels…receiving from one to several different monthly newsletters, tele-seminars and webinars, other resources, and invitation to two major international conferences annually, each typically attended by more than 1,000. Its most famous publication, *THE NO B.S. MARKETING LETTER,* is the most widely read paid-subscription newsletter on marketing in the world. We say that Glazer-Kennedy Insider's Circle™ is *The Place For Prosperity*™'cuz that sounds so good and has cool alliteration, and trademarks weren't available for our first four choices. For more information and membership invitation, visit www.DanKennedy.com. There are also 150 local Glazer-Kennedy Chapters and Kennedy Study/ Mastermind Groups meeting regularly in cities throughout the U.S. and Canada, and a directory can be found at www.DanKennedy.com.

FOR THE GREATEST FREE GIFT OFFER EVER

FROM GLAZER-KENNEDY INSIDER'S CIRCLE™, REFER TO PAGES III AND 241.

Our Official Company Motto

Money is better than poverty,
if only for financial reasons.

- Woody Allen

OTHER BOOKS BY THE AUTHOR, AS IF ANYBODY CARES

No B.S. Series—Entrepreneur Press

No B.S. *Business* Success for The New Economy

No B.S. *Sales* Success for The New Economy

No B.S. Wealth Attraction *for Entrepreneurs* – in The New Economy

No B.S. DIRECT Marketing for NON-Direct Marketing Businesses

No B.S. Ruthless Management of People and Profits

No B.S. Time Management *for Entrepreneurs*

Ultimate Sales Letter (Adams)

Ultimate Marketing Plan (Adams)

Make Millions With Your Ideas (Penguin)

No Rules (Plume)

Unfinished Business (Glazer-Kennedy/Advantage)

Secrets of Peak Performers (Glazer-Kennedy/Advantage)

Ultimate Success Secret (Kennedy/Lillo)

Why Do I Always Have To Sit Next To The Farting Cat? (Kennedy/Lillo)

The Last U.S. President's Last Speech/A Novel – (Smashwords.com)

> *"If you've written one book,*
> *you've written one book.*
> *If you've written two books, you're an author.*
> *If you've written more than twenty books,*
> *of course, you're a hack."*
>
> – Kinky Friedman

With co-authors

The New Psycho-Cybernetics – with Dr. M. Maltz (Prentice-Hall)

Zero Resistance Selling – with Dr. M. Maltz (Prentice-Hall)

Uncensored Sales Secrets – with Sydney Barrows (Entrepreneur Press)

Specialty titles

The Complete Moron's Guide to Typewriter Repair in the 21st Century (Halbert Press)

How To Take Title To Millions In Real Estate When The Owners Aren't Looking (LeGrand Books)

How To Profit In Your Future Lives (Milteer/Karma House)

How To Profit From The Positive Power of Pessimism, Cynicism And Despair (NSA Publishing)

IMPORTANT LEGAL NOTICES:

*It is mandated by federal law
that you read these notices
before continuing with this book.*

(1): It has been brought to our attention that there is another Dan S. Kennedy who is a published author, some sort of novelist. His books sometimes get mixed up with mine in listings at Amazon or elsewhere. This has caused him considerable consternation and put some money in lawyers' pockets. I want to state unequivocally that I am not he and he is not me – even though we've never been seen in the same room together at the same time. Whoever he is, he lays no claim to this book or any of my others, nor do I to his. In fact, I don't like his at all despite not having read them, but I like mine a great deal, despite not having read them. There is also a Dan Kennedy who owns a sales training company and lives in Scottsdale, Arizona. We were once both on an AmericaWorst flight from Phoenix to L.A. and I got there first so they canceled his ticket and fought him about boarding because he was already on board. This is the only time we met. I do not know him and he does not know me and we de not know anything about each other or endorse each other, although he admitted gaining some clients due to the confusion and I am unaware of any reciprocal benefit. There is also a speaker named Danielle Kennedy. She is taller than I am, and I am hotter. Finally, there is a Kennedy Fireplug Manufacturing Company in Ellwood, New Jersey. My products have been pissed on more than theirs. Anyway, that first guy is pissed off all the time about people confusing him with me. Try not to do it.

(2): This publication is not designed to provide accurate and authoritative information in regard to the subject matter covered, uncovered or not covered. It is sold or stolen, copied and sold cheap on eBay with the understanding that neither the author, his dog, or the publisher is engaged via this book in rendering legal, accounting, or other professional advice or services. Amateur at best. If such advice or expert assistance is required, the services of a competent professional should be sought. Under no circumstances should any business, career or romantic decisions be made based on your interpretations of the content of this book. Neither author nor publisher can be held liable for anything.

(3): Additional health warnings: if you read this book with your head inside a plastic bag sealed tightly around the base of your neck, it may very well seem funnier, but only briefly. Then you will die. And you will learn the truest and most clichéd lesson about comedy there is; dying is easy, comedy is hard. If this book bursts into flames while in your hands because you are struck by lightning while reading it, it's probably a message from somebody that ought not be ignored. If you read it at a pace of one page per day during lunch hour while consuming five Big Macs® for just $5, it will probably make you morbidly obese before you finish reading. Please do your reading at Starbucks instead, like a sophisticated person. Not any healthier, but I own stock in Starbucks. (That statement is not intended as an endorsement of Starbucks or its stock nor as investment opinion or advice. However, if enough of you reading this all bought a shitload of Starbucks stock on the same day then I could unload mine and I'd be very grateful.)

CONTENTS

AUTHOR'S INTRODUCTION

There's a scene in an episode of DEADWOOD that I **very much identify with**. It has the two competing gin mill and whorehouse owners standing side by side on a balcony overlooking the fledgling western town, one lamenting that the people are so damned dumb they can't learn to play roulette, the game he had just installed. The other owner says, "It *would* be easier to just hit 'em over the head, drag 'em out in the desert and take their money." The first "entrepreneur", thinking out loud, in a voice indicating mulling it over, slowly says "But that… would be…. *wrong*."

I laughed out loud like hell the first time I saw and heard it. You might not find it funny at all. And it may be unwisely revealing of myself to use it as an example. It illustrates that one man's funny is another man's not.

I first titled this book *'Mugging For Fun And Profit'*, then with a nod to *the* bestseller of the 60's, *'The Joy Of Mugging*.'* Then I decided nobody'd get those titles *but me*. So I wound up with *'Make 'Em Laugh And Take Their Money'.* Reminds of Napoleon Hill being threatened by his publisher with the title *'Use Your Noodle To Get The Boodle',* which Hill transformed to *'Think And Grow Rich.'* Overnight. The power of a deadline and desperation. Proves that every once in a while, an editor is good for something. Anyway, unless you *are* just going to hit 'em over the head and drag them out into the desert to empty their pockets, I'd suggest to you, you need to know how to make 'em laugh. **People buy more and buy more happily when in good humor**. But it's treacherous territory. It is not as easy as it looks, being funny, or even being amusing. One of the greatest sales copywriters of all time, Gary Halbert, once wrote screamingly funny "how fat are you?" radio ads for a weight loss company – that failed miserably. He forgot that fat is mostly, only funny if you're not. *(She was so fat small children gathered in her shadow for shade on hot days – and played jump-rope there. Hundreds of 'em.)* Incidentally, America IS fat. In fact – fact – Disneyland had to shut down the 'It's A Small World' ride and re-tool it in 2009 because the boats were sinking. The ride was built for butts 30 years ago. Today's walking wide loads weigh the little boats down so much they get stuck on the tracks and fill up with water. It's no longer a small world in southern California. But shaming fatties into buying, by ridiculing them still won't work. Nor will taxing soda pop.

This book is about humor purposed to support and facilitate persuasion, so that you need not drag them out into the desert and whack them unconscious before taking their wallets. They'll line up to hand their money to you.

*Sigh. The bestseller of the 60's was *Joy of Sex*. Its title a theft from the already, immensely popular book *Joy of Cooking*, reflecting an optimistic change in interests amongst America's housewives. Not long ago, a book titled *The Joy of Sleep* was published. Deduce what you will.

"Every fledgling speaker asks:
do you have to be funny?
Answer: only if you want to get paid."

- Robert Henry

Chapter 1

WHAT—AND QUIT SHOW BUSINESS?

es, *that* old joke: the guy visiting the circus sees the poor fellow in the elephant pen, knee deep in elephant shit, shoveling like mad, shirtless, sweating in the summer heat, gagging at the stench. The visitor says: "That looks like hell. Why don't you get a better job?" – to which the shit shoveler incredulously replies, "What? And give up show business?"

There are jokes everybody can see the end of before it arrives, that are still funny in some settings, to some people. A popular one from the Bill years: Bill Clinton walks off Air Force One carrying a pig under each arm. The waiting Secret Service agent politely says, "nice pigs, sir." President Clinton says, "Thank you. But these are not just pigs, son. These are authentic, genuine, purebred, prize-winning Arkansas Razorbacks. I got one for Hillary and one for Chelsea." And the deadpan Secret Service agent says: "Good trade, sir." Sure, you saw it coming. So what?

Anyway, back to quitting show biz. The day I decided to quit speaking, I was waiting in a hotel corridor to walk in and go on stage,

1

listening to my own introduction, when an amazing wave of dark dread came over me and I felt like running out the back door. I have the phobia that makes you want to leap from tall, open places like bridges or balconies and I have to be cautious of being in such places. It's an uncontrollable urge. I know what it feels like. And I felt it that day, as my legs were moving down the hall toward the exit instead of toward the entry to the stage. This wasn't about the arduous, life-draining travel and endless nights on the road and days in airports and old, cold, bad food; I'd grown to abhor that long before this moment. At this moment, I abhorred *the work*. I did not want to perform. I almost couldn't make myself perform. Still, quitting was no easy decision. I was at the top of that game, and my speaking schedule included 25 to 27 gigs a year on the biggest public seminar tour of all time. I was bringing in over a million dollars a year directly from speaking, my celebrity was entirely tied to speaking, and my business was fueled by and dependent on my speaking.

Many years ago, I was standing in a hallway listening to comedian Shelley Berman, from behind his locked hotel room door, insist he did not want to – no, *could not* – come out of his room and go to the theater and perform. I did not understand then. But when my moment in that hallway came, I understood perfectly. Even though I can't really explain it. I remember having the conversation about quitting with myself many times over months. Feeling worried and guilty about it. Looking in the mirror and saying: what, and give up show business?

But quit I did. (Making it 1000% unnecessary to keep ANYTHING about my speaking life to myself – thus the revealing of things here, in my 'Big Mouth, Big Money Program', in my other courses on the business of speaking –see the online catalog accessed via www. DanKennedy.com, and in one last – really, last – seminar I'm toying with doing about speaking.)

Of course, I still speak or, as I privately think of it, *perform** occasionally. As of this writing, at several GKIC events a year and, at most, several more. A far cry from the 50 to 70 gigs a year I did for about 15 years. The few I do now hardly count by comparison to the grind I was caught up in. And now that I don't feel like I have to, I find myself again enjoying being up there on stage, as much as one can.

(*By the way, too few entrepreneurs, shop-keepers, professionals, salespeople think of themselves as performers delivering performances every day. In the book I contributed a little to, mostly written by Sydney Barrows, *Uncensored Sales Secrets*, much is explained about selling as performance art, sales choreography, and sales language. You would be under more pressure if you viewed whatever you do as performance, but you'd also be a lot more successful at it.)

People often ask me if I was afraid of public speaking; so many people are. Or afraid of facing 500 or 5,000 or 25,000 people; the thought terrifies so many. I always tell them I never was, and that's the truth. I was never afraid of speaking to the audiences. But I was horrified at the thought of bombing. Not doing well, and I, do not get along. I do not respond well. I get angry to point of blood pressure boil-over, I get physically ill, I am morose and depressed, and beat myself up long and hard. So not doing well up there was, to me, an immense, enormous, 250 pound man standing on my chest, air gone from my lungs, painful pressure. The first relief came with the first good laugh. The ultimate and only accurate *measurement* was back of room sales. But the pressure let up and relief came with that first good, hearty, honest laugh from the crowd.

There have actually been few times I've gone out there and asked for that laughter and not gotten it. Those have been very, very bad times. An hour that lasts a year. Dying ever so slowly while standing up. 99% of the times the laughter has come. The relief has come. That laughter is air to a drowning man.

The ability to get those laughs, to make people relax and be uninhibited and enjoy you and themselves, to leave their worries behind and enter a different mind space, to feel a sense of shared, funny futility over life's problems and puzzles, to trust you enough to open up and laugh with you….. is as necessary to a performer or speaker as an audience itself. For the speaker seeking to sell, it is the golden key to the vault.

This does apply to persuasion by means other than public speaking too, and we'll get to that, here and there, throughout this book. But it is possible to persuade via media without ever eliciting a chuckle. It's nearly impossible to do it 'live', to a group, from the front of the room or the stage.

So this book is all about that. If it's laughter you're after, know that what I've shared in this book is a lifetime of work on the craft of getting that laughter, born of secret, sheer, utter desperation.

The Serious Work of Being Funny

Being funny is, ironically, serious business. People who are good at it work at it, just like people who are good at anything else.

Writing humor is harder than saying humor on stage, because the writer is deprived of body language, gestures, facial expression, props, and the peer pressure on the group by the early laughers and easy responders. Humorous writers from Parker and Benchley to contemporaries, Woody Allen, Dave Barry, Kinky Friedman accomplish something extraordinary when, purely with written words on pages, they make you laugh out loud. Only political speech-writers can match them, if unintentionally. Every direct-response advertising copywriter worth a damn or who aspires to be must; must; must study such humor writers, organize their stories for reference, and work at successfully incorporating both a good-natured, good-humored tone overall and good humorous stories that make sales points into their copy - because **people buy more and buy more happily when in good humor.**

But whether the written word or for use on stage or even for use one-to-one in selling, developing material that works is a lot of serious work. It is craftsmanship.

If I get a joke from somewhere I'm going to use on stage — or even just with friends — I work on it for a while. I tell it out loud to myself, changing out words, then fooling with voice inflections and timing, wondering which way sounds funnier. There's a dirty joke I got from Bobcat Golthwait that can only be told to male business owners, and cannot be cleaned up for use on stage. In its punchline you can use the word "bitch" or the more vile word "cunt". It is at least ten times funnier if you use the latter than the former, audience tested. I switched it from c-word to b-word when I got it but switched back after two tellings. Fortunately, a lot of dirty jokes can be cleaned up (Chapter 18) and still work. I say fortunately because there are more dirty jokes than clean ones. (Don't ask me to tell you this one. I have purged it from my subconscious files to prevent blurting it out when I shouldn't, and trashed the written version, so I won't be tempted to use it.)

It is more difficult, dangerous and necessary to be funny today than ever before in my lifetime. It is difficult because so much basis for humor is off limits: ethnic clichés and differences, for one. Except carefully about your own kind. Chris Rock can do material about blacks any white person would be lynched for, but ought not appear on stage in the south and do Foxworthy's *You Might Be A Redneck* material – or out might come the rope. And everything I just said is pretty much off limits. I shouldn't have said any of it. Lynching is suddenly a very sensitive topic again. A *politicized*, sensitive topic.

It is also difficult because peoples' exposure to professionally written and delivered comedy is constant – where once, short of physically going to performances, you would see a stand-up comic on Carson, here or there, now there are the HBO specials, the entire Comedy Channel, comedy clubs open nightly in every city, etc.

It is dangerous because one slip of tongue, one poorly chosen reference and you could be pilloried, sued, banished. Think Imus. He spent two years in exile on the Rural Farm Network before being let back in to real TV – but on Fox. I'm writing this just a few weeks before his reintroduction to society. Will he survive? Or be so cowed, so restricted, he won't be funny? After all, half his act has always been making fun of people. His slip-up was instructive; it was making fun of the wrong person. For example, Governor Sanford and his amazing trek on the Appalachian Trail to Argentina to consort with his mistress there – the outsourcing of yet one more American job – is fair game, but making fun of his aggrieved wife very, very dangerous territory indeed. Although her speed at moving from grief to having a book written and in stores and herself on the tears-and-sympathy talk show circuit almost as impressive as Sanford's accumulated frequent flier miles. She would have gotten there even faster if John Edwards' wife hadn't been in the way.

For all these and other reasons, humor is hard.

So, you might ask if it's just safer to avoid it altogether – in advertising, in sales copy, in speeches. Although he didn't mean for it to appear in this context, I'll let Zig Ziglar answer with his quote "Timid salesmen have skinny kids."

It is necessary because it is almost impossible to win over and influence audiences without it. Today, people are – more than ever – buying based on liking the person and enjoying their experience more than on merits of proposition. Even Ice Queen Hillary did her level best to be warmer, more human and, yes, funny during her 2008 campaign. And every politician now makes the rounds of comedy shows as well as the Sunday morning news shows, each attempting to diffuse unpopularity or suspicion; to create rapport and trust by being funny. During the health care reform fracas of late summer 2009, President Obama made himself the only guest on Letterman, and did his best with the woman in the audience named Apple who brought a potato shaped like I forget what – Andy Rooney? The Lincoln Memorial?, and gamely parried Dave's softest-ball queries with "Aw, shucks", a big grin, and lines written to get laughs. As salesman-in-chief of his administration, he pulled humor out of the sample case – not features 'n benefits. The greatest example of humor in selling in politics remains Reagan's, in the second debate with Mondale, after looking a bit feeble and confused in the first, thus making the issue of his age a real concern for the public and opportunity for his opponent. When Reagan did his head shake and delivered "Age should not be an issue in this campaign. I am not going to make my opponent's youth and inexperience an issue…" and got a laugh from the audience *and from Mondale*, it was all over but counting up the margin of victory.

Another reason you really can't afford timid safety and need humor in selling today is that attention spans keep getting shorter. Trying to get anybody to even focus on a sales pitch so it can sell is an increasingly difficult task. Their little minds have been turned to mush by constant, multi-sourced, multi-sensory stimulation. Constant connectedness to tweets and texts and cell phone yakking and high speed video games and hopping about on internet. One study showed the average length of time a visitor who goes to *The New York Times* web site stays there is 2 minutes 17 seconds. *The New York Times*. What could you possibly glean from it in 2 minutes 17 seconds? Well, for better or worse, **people will give**

more minutes of attention to something they find entertaining and amusing than they will to anything serious. To sell whatever it is you sell, however you sell it, to the max, you are in show biz. So you might as well get good at it.

Chapter 2

WHAT'S FUNNY?

We'll list some of what's funny here. Get into depth in subsequent chapters. But first, some bad news. Few things are *inherently* funny. Visual humor – a monkey smoking a cigar, a squirrel surfboarding, a man – preferably a fat man slipping on a banana peel. But beyond

"I'M SORRY SIR, THERE'S NO SMOKING ON THIS FLIGHT. AND YOU'RE GOING TO HAVE TO PUT ON PANTS!"

Vincent Palko
www.AdToons.com

'Funniest Videos', what's funny from the platform is made funny from the platform. So if you're hoping you can find things that are funny to carry your water for you, they're in short supply. A monkey smoking a cigar is that, but traveling with him a real pain in the ass.

There, are, however, **categories** of source material to work from, in which to find good fodder for humor:

Stupidity. People laugh at stupid criminals, stupid politicians, stupidity in their own industry or field, and stupid shared experiences. A perfect example is Lewis Black's bit about the nuclear attack drills all of us children of the 50's went through at school....where, with a giant *flaming* ball of atomic Armageddon roaring toward us, we were told to seek refuge *under our desks*. Little *wood* desks. Black says it was at that moment he decided never to pay any attention to instructions from authority figures again. That piece of business works as pure humor because it showcases stupidity: the stupidity of government, of educators, and of our own silly behavior. This same bit could be used by the speaker to not only get laughs and get an audience on his side with shared experience, but also to connect to any number of points. You could connect it to taking a poke at corporate management (always popular with the troops) or to highlight the virtues of independent thought. I might point out, though, this is made funnier by good delivery than it is written on the printed page, and I italicized those words for a reason.

Rants. People like angry comics who are mad at the shared stupidity and aggravations everybody suffers. The rant-er is saying what everybody wants to say. Dennis Miller made his career with rants.... *"I don't want to go off on a rant here, but..."*. Sam Kinison's very, very angry and bitter rant about the women who broke his heart and took his money expressed most men's private thoughts and emotions, so they cheered on his rage. You don't have to go to Sam's extremes to use a rant. Talking about what ticks you off about airline travel...voice mail hell...bad customer service...employees....or some 'enemy' of your particular audience in a humorous way will work just fine and can be linked to points for a selling argument. You may have heard or read my often used rant about cell phones, centered on idiot men talking on them while simultaneously standing at urinals and peeing. I also incorporate little rants in sales copy I write for myself or clients, and in my opening monologues in the *No B.S. Marketing Letter*, in my books, and in my political columns published at BusinessAndMedia.org. I've included little rants in sales copy I write for myself or clients, and in my opening monologues in the *No B.S. Marketing Letter*, in my books, and in my political columns published at BusinessAndMedia.org. I've included some examples in Appendix I of this book. If you're a reasonably alert human with an IQ above 12 and you at least occasionally leave your house, there must be things that really piss you off. You probably rant about them now, to spouse, friends, dog or – if you live alone and are a certain sort of person, your plants. Your rant is likely repetitive too. Just get it down on paper and then make it funny.

Shared, Common Experiences. In speaking or writing to persuade, you are seeking rapport and trust. Nothing gets you there better than shared life experiences. Sure, if you and your prospect, reader or audience share, say, Midwest upbringing, that provides a certain level of automatic rapport. But if you can good-naturedly describe the putting away of all the summer clothes in basement or attic, the dragging out of the big, bulky winter clothes, and her switching to her big, bulky, flannel and wool pajamas so that the curve of female anatomy disappears from view at home or abroad from November until May; if you can speak to the fish sticks on Fridays doled out by the gigantic cafeteria lady with the snaggle tooth and hair net...or the never-ending road projects, the hundreds of thousands of orange traffic cones blocking off miles and miles of roadway, narrowing to one lane of bumper to bumper traffic, with no one actually working on the road anywhere in sight – only one sadist with day-glo vest and shovel to lean on as he watches you creep, creep, creep by....you get a leg up with fellow Midwesterners.

> *"My wife is an interior decorator. She wants to get rid of me because I clash with the drapes."*
>
> *- Morey Amsterdam*

The shared experience is love and marriage – 52% of the average audience is married, another 30% divorced or moving toward marriage in a relationship. Everybody gets it. And everybody has the same experiences, the same frustrations with each other. The war of the thermostat. The same argument conducted with the exact same out-come for 20 years. *Tip: just assign it a number. You say #36, I say #36, and that's the end of it.*

I tell audiences that were it not for the institution of marriage, golf would never have been invented. Think about it: men volunteering to walk miles up and down hills to whack at a tiny ball with sticks trying to do the impossible and drive the ball into a tiny, distant hole. The same guy who's just too exhausted to take a bag of trash out Friday night is up at 6:00 A.M. Saturday morning for a long walk in the woods, in the rain, dragging a bag of sticks. Who's kidding who?

Golf was invented by married men as the only way to get out of the house their wives would allow – because it seems to gals like stupidity, which they believe systemic with husbands, and misery, which they like inflicting on husbands – they know we've done *something* to deserve punishment even if they aren't sure what it is.

See, if four guys tell their wives they want to go hang out with their buddies at the strip club for four hours to smoke cigars, drink, and tell filthy jokes and complain about their wives, who's getting out of the house? But if four guys tell their wives they want to lug a bag of heavy sticks around for four hours, frantically trying to hit little balls up hills into little holes only to come home pissed off and embarrassed and tired, they say "Have a nice time, dear."

You can deliver that 'soft', sort of conversational, in fun, or as a rant. Either way it works.

If you want to connect it to something, you have choices – for example, how we invent cumbersome, complicated, frustrating ways of doing things in our businesses too. Pogo said, "We have met the enemy and they is us", the bridge from such a story, to the making of things more difficult than they need be and making ourselves miserable in the process, to the solution you offer, your easy-button, your pleasant, utopian 'walk unspoiled.'

"After we have sex but before I kill you, I'm going to need your help with some shelves."

© Joe Dator/Condé Nast Publications/www.cartoonbank.com

THIS IS FROM AN INTERVIEW in *Cigar Aficionado Magazine* with actor/Paul Harvey stand-in/ former Senator/briefly, presidential candidate Fred Thompson and his considerably younger wife Jeri, in their home…

...Jeri is asked about Thompson's shortcomings as a husband. She smiles and without hesitation, says, "There's not a lot of help around the house. It just doesn't occur to him."

Thompson, seemingly absorbed in his salad, doesn't miss a beat. Looking up, he says, deadpan, *"I resent that,"* pauses, then offers the zinger. "It *does* occur to me. Don't confuse lack of awareness with the lack of willingness to do something about it."

And there is very old, very evergreen material about marriage finding its way into what I'm guessing is a polished comedy act by this pair, she the straight-man, he the wit. Circa 2009. Wives have been complaining about husbands not doing anything around the house since everybody lived in caves, and cartoonists and comedians have used it since the first cave dweller's stand-up act the original Improv.

Kids offer shared experience humor, too. Thanks to Catholics still relying on the rhythm method and the difficulty of getting an orchestra into the bedroom at 3:00 A.M. (bada-boom. Sorry. *Dad's* joke.) and an apparent shortage of condoms plus marriage or other relationship arrangements seem to produce kids. Even Britney Spears was able to produce some. So just about everybody has 'em or has had 'em, or at least hangs around people who have 'em. Art Linkletter, who I had the pleasure of working with a bit in 2007, made himself famous with his TV shows and books – *"Kids Say The Darndest Things."* Every issue of *Readers Digest* includes at least several amusing stories of parents and kid trouble. *Dennis The Menace* is one of the longest running, if not the longest running, newspaper comic in America. It has endured while countless others have come and gone, despite lacking any edginess whatsoever, because it represents universally shared experience.

Pets, another opportunity. They are the new kids, and while they may have an 'accident' in the house, they rarely need bailed out of jail or require mortgaging your house for their four year degree in feminist studies and philosophy. Most people know somebody who spoils their dog or cat, if they're not guilty themselves, so when I talk about our Million Dollar Dog, everybody identifies and is amused by my silly behavior. As you may know, the Million Dollar Dog does not stay in an ordinary kennel i.e. prison camp when we travel. She usually stays at The Barkley Pet Hotel and Spa. Get it? BARK-ly. There are four choices of private suites to choose from including those with pool view, dinners from menu – including steak delivered from a near-by Morton's, TV's, optional limo rides to get some fresh air, and, of course, play time. Unfortunately, the Million Dollar Dog, originally Carla's and graced with her pleasant personality, has, since hanging around me, become just a bit territorial. No longer plays well with others. Flunked the required initial evaluation by the doggie shrink and is not permitted to go to doggie day camp with the other visiting pups. So we must pay for her extra private play-times. Belly rubs. And reading of a bedtime story and tucking in. If I could fit in the 'suite', I'd consider checking myself into this place the next time Carla goes out of town. At a certain age, perhaps permanently.

The Million Dollar Dog didn't start out as such, but the little princess has become pretty high maintenance since Carla and I got back together and I started spoiling the little furball. She even has her own leopard-print couch with two matching pillows, about $800.00. She now knows the difference between the approach to the regular airport terminal or the turn-off to the private terminal, and lets her objection to the first be heard. She prefers strolling up onto the plane, getting treats from the pilots and having her choice of seats.

Everybody can appreciate these Million Dollar Dog stories. Whether they think the stories are exaggerated for effect or not doesn't matter. And just for the record, they're not. Last week, the Million Dollar Dog called a family meeting and brought her lawyer, to talk about our wills. With the full support of Obama's nut-case Science Czar, who has actually advocated, in writing, that animals be represented by attorneys and welcomed in court with lawsuits against people. Trees, too.

If you pick up a starving dog and make him prosper, he will not bite you. This is the principal difference between a man and a dog.

- Mark Twain

TWEETS FROM THE MILLION DOLLAR DOG

9:45 A.M.   My people have been making too much noise so I have gotten up. My dish is empty. This is not starting well.

10:20 A.M.   That big, bushy-haired brown thing they call a squirrel has dared to come into my lawn behind my deck. I have barked and chased the little bugger back into the woods where he belongs. Now, where's my treat?

11:40 A.M.   My nap has been disturbed by the big guy lumbering up from the basement, but it's okay. He does this about this time everyday and gets food, and I sit and eat with him.

12:10 P.M.   I have raced downstairs and barked and reminded the big guy to feed that gray box-shaped animal in the corner. It eats paper. I like to chew paper but I wouldn't eat it. To each his own.

12:45 P.M.   I have checked on my main dog feeder person in her office and she seems fine.

1:20 P.M.   I have just taken a well-earned, very satisfying dump.

2:40 P.M.   That damn squirrel disturbed my afternoon nap. Eternal vigilance.

4:10 P.M.   I am waiting at the top of the stairs for the big guy. It is past play time. He's got a hundred clocks down there, you'd think he could get up here on time.

4:25 P.M.   Play time.

6:00 P.M.   Dinner. Seems like I have to remind them everyday.

6:30 P.M.   I'm taking my people out for a walk. The Million Dollar Dog's work is never done.

Anybody can develop and productively use shared experience humor. It happens all around you, everyday. If you have kids or pets or annoying neighbors or got snookered into trying to win a stuffed bear at a carnival ring toss game and $412.00 later collapsed from exhaustion only to see an 8 year old *girl* hit three for three on her first try or have been on every goofy diet you can name and actually *gained* weight eating cabbage soup and tofu Pop Tarts, you've got plenty of material. It just has to be developed. You match it up with a sales point you can use, work backwards from that point to structure and perfect and polish the story, write it out, memorize it, and you've got schtick.

Maybe the most interesting humor, though, is in the category of *guilty* laughter – the stuff people feel guilty laughing at, but do. This is a unique kind of shared experience itself. We see or hear something we know we're not supposed to find funny, but we do.

Woody Allen had a story in his old stand-up act about going to pick up a girl for a first date, and waiting in her apartment's small living room while she finished getting ready. Waiting with her little dog. Bored, he found a ball, bounced it; the dog fetched it; again; again; then, too much on the ball, it bounced right out the window – and the dog gamely followed it. From twenty-eight floors up. If you tell this you will see people, mostly women, horrified at this tale. You will see disapproving looks on their faces. The punch line is: the woman comes out ready to go and Woody says, "You know, your dog seemed *a little depressed.*" The same people who were horrified laugh or chuckle. Guiltily.

Woody's joke is a sophisticated version of a joke Zig Ziglar skillfully used for years, that also created slightly guilty laughter. People knew it was insensitive, but it was funny. It's the one about the neighbor asked to watch over the other's house, feed the pet cat and even check on Grandma while they were away for a few days. The cat escaped and was run over by a car. When calling in to check on things, the neighbor was told "Cat's dead." The horrified caller said, "Oh my God! You couldn't have broken that to me more gently? You could have told me the cat ran out the door, and up a tall tree. How you tried to get the cat down. How it leapt over to the roof. Slipped on a loose tile. Fell out into the street." After a pause, the neighbor then asked, "Well, how's Grandma?"

"She's...... on the roof."

To construct jokes, you need to see that Zig's joke and Woody's joke are the same joke. It gets the same sort of response. And either could be used with persuasive purpose.

Let me make that point about structure again. Just as direct-response copywriters rely on certain formulaic structures for ads or sales letters, such as problem-agitate-solve or attention-interest-desire-action, comedy writers have their own portfolio of stock, off the shelf structures for jokes and stories. If you are going to create humor for your own purposes, you need to grow familiar with these common structures and be able to fit your own ideas or experiences to them. The structure of the joke told by Woody and the joke told by Zig might best be described as build-up with common, ordinary experience everyone can identify with + things suddenly go badly awry + awkwardly insensitive response by person caught in the tragedy. Abbreviated:

ordinary experience/disaster/inappropriate response. So, who hasn't been tasked with watching somebody's house, kid or pet and had chaos or disaster ensue? Who hasn't had a first date head south early? This, incidentally, is the comedy structure behind the entire *Curb Your Enthusiasm* show on HBO, put together by and starring the hapless Larry David as himself. It is also the foundation of a popular series of funny TV commercials used throughout 2009 by Southwest Airlines, all ending with the question: want to get away? One shows a person snooping in a medicine cabinet and having all the shelves suddenly collapse, noisily spilling everything out onto the floor with a crash. Who hasn't snooped in a medicine cabinet? Who hasn't had some embarrassing event occur, when they just wanted to get away?

My Franz-the-circus-midget story gets the same sort of reaction. Growing horror. Guilty laughter. That little bit of schtick came, by the way, courtesy of an actual news report on CNN, and my immediate, inappropriate thoughts about it being funny. Quickly jotting them down. Thank you CNN, and my condolences to Franz' family.

These kind of jokes are a way of letting the audience into a wink-and-nod with you, a conspiracy of sorts; that, together, today or tonight, we're going to be *a little* naughty, *a little* insensitive, *a little* politically incorrect in our examination of the human condition. It's a way of bonding.

When Larry The Cable guy tells one of these, he challenges his audience with – "I don't care who you are, now, that's funny", or he lowers his head in mock sorrow, saying "Oh my God. I'm sorry. I shouldn't have said that. It's just not right." By about the third or fourth time he trots that out, the audience is on to him, and laughs as soon as he starts it. Larry is, incidentally, a gimmick comic, in that his character is wholly fabricated and not him. His name isn't Larry, he's never worked as a cable repairman, and he's not a hick. He *is* one of the richest comedians, period.

Pie In Somebody Else's Face Is Funny

A special kind of humor-we-ought-not-laugh-at-but-do is the situation that's funny only when it happens to the other guy.

When Pete Lillo (PeteThePrinter.com) called to tell me his tale of woe, of a flooded basement, ruined documents and computers, renting of pumps and so forth. I said: if it had to happen to one of us, better you than me. Joan Rivers, of whom I am an enormous fan, even more so after working with her, admits that, walking down a New York street near ground zero the day after 9-11, she was thinking of jokes and how soon it might be possible to use them. The first thing this reveals is that people who are funny *think funny*. Compulsively. We see comedy in just about everything, even when others would judge it wholly inappropriate.

Second, it reveals a fundamental truth: tragedy is comedy. Sometimes separated from itself by time. Sometimes when it happens to the other guy. Comedy and tragedy are very close kin, and there are only these two things separating them from each other: time, and who is at the receiving end.

There are few dark incidents for which humor can never be accepted. 9-11 might just be one of them. But deadly wildfires in California wiping out peoples' homes and treasured belongings have been fodder for jokes by Leno, a very un-edgy, deliberately gentle and likeable personality. The tragic series of events that led to the destruction of a much admired sports hero's life; the violent murders of two people; finally, the disgraced hero engaged in a stupid incident in which he and a room full of scumbags fought over his memorabilia, leading to his sentence to 8+ years in prison, this no comedian has even thought twice about reveling in – yet tragedy it is and has been.

EXAMPLES OF COMEDY STRUCTURES & TYPES OF JOKES

Question/Answer. How Fat Was She? She Was So Fat That_____. Egs: *How cold is it? It was so cold in Central Park that I saw squirrels with frost on their nuts.* (That's ancient, but Letterman used it this year.)

Switch. A story appearing to head in one direction, that switches abruptly at punch line. Egs.: *A son says to his mother: "I don't want to go to school today. No one at school likes me. The kids make fun of me. The teachers shun me. I don't want to go." His mother says: "You have to go. You're not sick. You have no excuse. And you're 46 years old and you're the principal."* To use that, you would put a lead-in in front of it: Egs.: Sometimes we all have things we just don't want to do, right? Like the son telling his mother…. – and afterward, you'd bridge from it to your point: maturity is doing things we don't necessarily like or feel like doing in order to pursue objectives we really want. Another egs.: *My husband is a wiz at fixing things around the house. Saturday he fixed six martinis.*

Chain-of-If's. This was a very common structure used by humorous writers in the 30's and 40's. Egs: *I had dinner last night at that new gourmet restaurant. If the oysters had been as ice-cold as the soup, if the soup had been as warm as the wine, if the wine as old as the chicken, and if the chicken as young as the waitress, it would have been terrific.* Egs.: *I found this Post-It Note on the Bible in the hotel nightstand drawer: If in trouble, see Psalm 50, verse 15. If unhappy, Ecclesiastes 7:3. If lonesome, Jeremiah 29:13. If still lonesome, call 416-8740 and ask for Bambi.*

Count Me Out'isms. The most famous of these is Groucho Marx's "I do not wish to belong to any club that would have me as a member." Robert Benchley claimed to have applied to his bank for a loan, been approved and promptly closed all his accounts, saying "How could I trust my money with a bank that would make a loan to somebody like me?"

Definitions – Alternate Definitions. Egs.: *The consummate negative thinker is: a person who smells fresh flowers and immediately start looking around for the coffin.* Egs. of alternate definition: *Everybody knows that M.B.A. stands for More Bad Advice. But there's a new designation: MBA-WAS. Stands for an MBA who's Working At Starbucks.*

Allusive Quotation. A familiar saying attributed (without regard to accuracy) to a historical or famous figure, that association providing the humor. Egs.: *As Methuselah said, 'The first hundred years are the toughest.' Or was it Joan Rivers who said that? I forget.*

Analogy. I swiped these from Bob Orben to describe the manufacturing company I once ran: *No two snowflakes are exactly alike. We have a production line with that same problem. It's hard to describe our operation – picture a nervous breakdown with paychecks.*

Up-Dated Situations. Egs.: *They just don't make Westerns like they used to. That new one out in the theaters is a disappointment. The bandits rob the stage, get caught, beat the rap in court because they weren't properly read their rights. Then they're tried and convicted on tax evasion.*

News Bulletins. Fake headlines or news stories. On stage, can be read from notes taped inside newspapers and magazines, providing props and relieving need for memorization. Another way to use the gag is with "this just in" news reports occurring throughout a speech or seminar – they can be brought to you by a messenger, or have yourself interrupted by announcer on the P.A. system.

One-Liners. The King of One-Liners was comedian Henny Youngman, and if you're serious about using them, you need to track down a Henny Youngman jokebook. One-line jokes. Just punch lines. Hardest for non-pros to write and make work. Often delivered one right after the other by pro comedians. Egs. of mine: *I was raised Lutheran – that's Catholic without confession. We gave up saints for Lent.* Short person's: *I failed to make the high school chess team because of my height.* And from the great Henny Youngman: *"The horse I bet on was so late getting home, he tip-toed into the stable."*

Optimist's Statement. Optimism (and pessimism) has been the basis for humor forever. The simplest use is a single sentence or answer given by the overt optimist. Egs. from Mark Victor Hansen: *"I went in to get a loan. The banker asked for my statement. I said I was optimistic."*

Optimist-Pessimist. Structure is simple – what one says, what the other says. Egs.: *The pessimistic business owner was whining about how bad things had gotten – "so bad I can't even pay my bills." The optimist said, "Well, there's something to be thankful for, that you're not one of your creditors."* Egs.: *Two partners owned the store, one an optimist, the other a pessimist. The store's Saturday had been a record-breaker. "Gotta tell ya," the optimist says, "we've had more customers through here today than in any good week before." Pessimist says: "Yeah, and if it keeps up, we'll have to replace the damn door hinges and the carpet'll be worn out in no time."*

Paradox. A statement in conflict with itself. Egs.: *The President said: I am committed that, from now on, this government will live within our means – even if we have to borrow to do it.* Longer egs.:

They want you buy an airline ticket to fly to California, and stay in a pricey resort for 3 days to attend a $3,000.00 metaphysical seminar titled 'There's More To Life Than Money.'

Quadrigrams. Four ideas, observations or instructions tied together. Egs.: *Go to experts for assistance, to friends for sympathy, to strangers for charity, and to relatives – for nothing.* Egs.: *Magicians can live without air for minutes. Camels can go without water for days. Bears can go months without food. He's been able to go his entire life without ideas.*

Who's The Boss? – Marriage Jokes. Egs.: *Guy's interviewing a new executive assistant, and she's fabulous. Can type at lightning speed with no errors, speaks three languages, used to be a travel agent, she's perfect – except she also looks like Angelina Jolie. He says: "you've got the job – if you've got a really bad driver's license photo I can show my wife." At a party months later, she introduces herself to the wife – "I'm his executive assistant." Tom's wife says: "Oh, were you?"* Egs: *The best way to tell if a man is having fun at a party is to look at his wife's face.*

Skeptic's Comeuppance. This can be particularly useful for motivational/business speakers. The set-up has someone pitching an idea, a product, etc.; the skeptic reacts badly; the end has the idea man victorious. An old favorite of mine: *Guy goes to see the Hollywood talent agent on audition day. The agents says : "Okay, kid, what do you do?" Guy says he does the best bird imitations of* *anybody who's ever set foot on stage. The agent tells him that Ed Sullivan is dead, there's no place for a bird imitator's act, and to get the hell out of the office. At which point the guy flies out the window.*

Time/Place, Mocked. A lot of humor comes from making fun of a place – the small town you grew up in, the place you just visited, etc. – and it is often done by using time. Egs.: *They move very slowly in the Bahamas. Takes a bit of adjusting. If you ask somebody what time it is, he says: June.* Egs.: *I spent a year in that town one weekend.* Egs.: *Alaska. Guy on trial there for murder gets asked: and where were you on the night of October 23rd to March 4th?* Lewis Black's bit about the long flight to Australia is this.

Twisted Proverbs. Egs: *Edison proved that the road to success is paved with good inventions.* Egs.: *If you give a man a fish, you feed him for a day. If you teach a man to fish, you create a new customer for Cabela's.* Egs.: *Familiarity breeds.* **Story/joke with Twisted Proverb as punch line.** *Egs.: I was briefly a boxer. After getting beaten to a pulp and almost killed, my manager said: don't worry about this. I'll get you a re-match if it's the last thing you do.*

Famous Persons' Mallapropisms & Twisted Proverbs. Egs.: From Yogi Berra: *"When you come to a fork in the road, take it."* From Sam Goldwyn: *"It's an impossible situation, but it has possibilities."*

Embellishment. Taking something that actually happened and turning it into a "tall tale", enhanced with details and exaggerations to make it funny. My house-on-fire story in my basic, million dollar speech selling Magnetic Marketing is example.

Exaggerations. Egs.: *My new puppy is so smart, while I was paper training him, he learned to read.*

Dark Comedy. Usually short jokes about murder, death, disaster with punch lines as likely to get gasps as laughs. Egs.: *"I was married twice," the guy told the man next to him at the bar. "My first wife dead from eating poison mushrooms." The other fellow acknowledges that was a horrible tragedy, then asks about his second wife. "She died too. From a fractured skull. Which she got when – she wouldn't eat her mushrooms."*

Unlikely Situations. Mike Vance's story about the nun on the bobsled. Usually, structurally, the entire situation described is ridiculous, then there's a punch line of final absurdity. Woody Allen's story about accidentally hitting a moose while en-route to a costume party, dressed as a moose; tying the moose to the fender; it coming to, coming into the party, and losing the costume contest to another person in a moose costume. Lenny Bruce used to tell a story about a child abandoned by his parents in Yellowstone National Park, raised by a pack of wild dogs, found, years later, walking on all fours and eating raw meat…rescued…put in school where he shocked the world by breezing through, graduating high school early, going to college and getting his Ph.D. – but tragically dying the day he graduated. Killed – *chasing a car.*

Comedy Has Context

Comedy has context. A guy slipping on a banana peel is funny. People have laughed at it for 100 years. Will tomorrow. It's funny to everybody but the guy slipping on it. You can show a film clip at a seminar of one person after another slipping on a peel, wildly flailing about and crashing, sliding, flopping to the ground and the audience will roar with laughter. Or you could show video clips of 'sports bloopers': race car crashes, or people being thrown off uncooperative horses, and get big laughs. Unless you did it at a program where Christopher Reeve was speaking. Then it's not funny at all. But 'it' didn't change. The context did.

I spoke on about 30 or 35 events where the paralyzed, wheelchair-confined 'Superman'-actor Christopher Reeve spoke. I was very happy that there was always one or two speakers after him, between him and me. Without their buffer, I'd have had a much tougher time doing what I did at the very beginning, to stop the mass exit of the audience with humor, and to get going with humor. He made just about all humor inappropriate if immediately following him. But video of people slipping and falling *definitely* would have been inappropriate.

Only a few things stay off limits forever. Sam Kinison is the only stand-up comic I've ever heard do JFK jokes – and rather viscious ones. 40 years after the fact, JFK is not funny. Clinton, however, is the Rodney Dangerfield of Presidents. He gets no respect. You can say he threw away right to it himself. But you could also do jokes about pretty much the same behavior in both Presidents, although JFK had better taste. And, as far as we know, his activities involved no Cuban cigars. Cuba yes, but no cigars. Tragic death is therefore a context, as is enduring popularity with the public.

Race makes certain things dangerous. You can make fun of Sarah Palin for goofy, witless remarks, and outright call her stupid – and offend only diehard conservative supporters of hers. But if you do the same with Barack Obama, say for his assertion that if we all just kept our tires properly inflated, there'd be no need to drill for oil and our energy crisis would be solved, or for his umbilical cord connected to tele-prompters, and you run risks beyond offending; you risk being presumed and labeled a racist. Race, therefore, is a context.

> *"There's something*
> ### *dangerous*
> *about what's funny.*
> *Jarring and disconcerting.*
> *There is a connection*
> *between funny and scary."*
>
> *- Christopher Walken*

Another context is what the audience expects from you and how they relate to you. Rickles' act is dangerous by today's standards, but Rickles is beloved by his audiences; they know what to expect; they go in hopes of being insulted. We went to see the big, tall guy from *Everybody Loves Raymond* in Las Vegas and to our dismay found he'd stolen Rickles' act and did it dirtier and more viciously, with less humanity. Worse, none of us expected anything like it from him. We didn't laugh much. We were uncomfortable. We left with a bad taste in our mouths.

In my world, it's never *just* about getting laughs. That's easier than what I do, and what you probably need to do. If all you want is an audience convulsed in laughter, you can work dirty. Or you can just deliver schtick, like "You Might Be A Redneck If" – with no concern whatsoever about offending anybody in the audience who does live in a trailer park or who does come from Appalachia. Or you can do fat chick jokes like Larry The Cable Guy, and if there are a few overweight women and their husbands sacrificed in a crowd of a thousand, so what? But we use humor for the purpose of advancing a sale, for the purpose of persuading people to embrace certain ideas, so the risk of offense or alienation has to be considered, and whether or not the humor moves the case being made forward has to be top priority.

For us, there is that extra context to consider – the context of the sales presentation. With rare exception, nothing belongs in a sales presentation that doesn't somehow advance the making of the sale. You can't just stick your favorite story in because it's your favorite story and you tell it well; it has to contribute to the making of the sale you are tasked with making. Obviously, then, anything that might detract or distract from advancing the sale almost certainly does not belong and needs jettisoned or avoided. Figuring out what's funny and then writing or talking about it in a funny way is important, but, while a comedian's job may stop with that, ours does not. We must figure out what's funny *and* that can be used to advance the sale *and* does not distract from or endanger the sale, then write or talk about it in a funny way that advances the sale and does not distract from or endanger the sale.

WHAT'S FUNNY ABOUT **THIS?**

THERE'S A SPOT in my Al The Plumber story* where, after describing him in suit, carrying attaché case, I say that nothing about him resembles a plumber except the little cloth patch sewn on his suit coat pocket *that says Al.* That always gets a laugh. I've never been sure that I understand why.

But as soon as it did, I altered the voice inflection and pauses to give it even more emphasis – and it gets bigger laughs. That's one of the things you have to do as a speaker using humor: try things out and let the audience tell you what they find funny. Anytime they do, then work on that little bit of material and the way you deliver it to make it funnier. (*See, pages 382-386 of *My Unfinished Business,* Glazer-Kennedy/Advantage edition.)

Chapter 3

THE FUNNIEST THING ON EARTH IS IN THE MIRROR

For his show *Curb Your Enthusiasm*, Larry David has presented himself as us all at our worst. We are all occasionally clueless, boorish, clumsy, insulting, rude; we all put our feet in our mouths now and then; we all get into a hole and keep digging, making our situation worse by the minute. If we could step out of body and watch and hear ourselves, we'd cringe. I cringed so much watching the show, I stopped watching it despite its genius. This entire show is self-deprecation and self-depreciation on parade. To such extreme, I can't imagine it making him endearing to many. In a way, his invention is magnification of early Woody Allen, from movies like *Annie Hall*. And we did find him endearing. But Larry? No.

Self-deprecating humor (but not self-depreciating humor) can be endearing and very effective in humanizing the speaker/writer, authority figure, expert, etc. so that rapport and trust are established. It can be used to balance out necessary bragging or preaching or dictatorial ordering about, all needed in selling.

So first, the difference between self-deprecating and self-depreciating. It's important. Most dictionaries treat these as synonyms, but they're wrong.

We Are All Idiots At Times

Self-deprecating humor is about shared humanity. Letting the audience in on "I'm human too". It's usually about you doing silly or embarrassing things, being taken down a peg by someone or something. Being caught in a situation that makes you look foolish. Ideally the stories used involve situations everybody can identify with, imagine themselves doing the same foolish thing or at least something like it. Many speakers tell – as I do - some version of the "do you know who I am?" story, or the "search for cuff-links" story, both gently self-deprecating. I make fun of my age, talking about the lovely young thing approaching me, book in hand, for an autograph – then asking me to write it out to her mother, who's my biggest fan. It was Lee Milteer who first, very coldly observed that my groupies seem to be getting a lot older. Of course, we're all getting older and few of us are getting better-looking as we go. And most people start getting sensitive about age when they turn 40, really touchy at 50. So if you're talking or writing to folks of that age group, your own discomfort with baldness, waking up with a sports injury apparently obtained while *sleeping*, or having hot babes ask you for autographs for their grand-mothers (*it will so brighten her day in that dreary nursing home!*), puts you and them in it together, on the same page. The same material with an audience of 30 year olds is worthless and potentially harmful.

> *"I'll tell you something*
> *about good-looking people.*
> *We're not well-liked."*
>
> *- Larry David*

Self-depreciating material, however, is best avoided by anybody trying to maintain status and stature in order to sell. Stories or jokes about self in this category actually depreciate your value. Any story that might cast doubt on your integrity, for example, should never be used. Or a story that might leave the impression you are mean-spirited. So, for example Seinfeld's material about marriage and his bumbling about within the institution would be fine for any of us, Ron White's material about his frustrations in marriage funnier but ill-advised for us, Andrew Dice Clay's material absolutely out of bounds for us – even if we were speaking to an all-male audience. On that scale, you move from good-natured to mean to vicious. As you move that way, you actually diminish yourself. Meanness or bitterness can get laughs, but it immediately leaves a sour after-taste. **Generally speaking, people buy from likeable people they like.** You must also take care with your "before" stories – about being poor, dumb and broke, failing, fat, whatever. There's a great deal of good humor to be found in such experience, but you must be sure to tie it to an "after" of rainbows and happiness, so it does not leave you depreciated in authority.

I have to be careful with all my schtick about being a luddite, stubbornly unconnected to the internet, Twitter, Facebook or even cell phones. It is embellishment of truth, and it is a rich source of humorous material, but it risks self-deprecation; having myself seen as unqualified to advise on marketing by being so out of it. When I use this anti-techno stuff, I always have to qualify it by making it known I make a great deal of money having the technology/media used for me, I get results there for clients, and I know more than I let on. Confidentially, I know *a lot* more than I let on. I know how to change a spark-plug too, but that doesn't mean I'm willing to have anything to do with anything under the hood of my car. You do know, rabies-infected demons live there, don't you?

In short, you have to be careful to crossing over from self-deprecating to self-depreciating. One can be very useful, the other is dangerous and can be very damaging. With that caution said, it is true that nothing, nothing, nothing can get the audience on your side better than self-deprecating humor. On a Glazer-Kennedy Insider's Circle™ call for Diamond Members, Frank Kern even made the point that somebody with no natural humor whatsoever, and who appeared humorless – say a C.P.A. with an M.B.A. – could be funny by making fun of how unfunny he was and was going to be. It's a good point. You never want to actually apologize to an audience, but this fellow could tell them of his being asked by his wife to practice his speech for her on nights she's unable to get to sleep, or tell the audience of the warning on the CD's of his speeches: not to be listened to while driving or operating heavy machinery. This will lower expectations and, then, if he happens to be not deadly dull and boring, they'll think he's better than he is. Early in his career, Bob Newhart used this ploy to his benefit. He was an accountant, was introduced as an accountant turned comedian, and walked out on stage blandly dressed looking like an accountant, and peoples' natural reaction was "uh-oh, this guy's gonna put us all into a coma". When he was funny, the surprise made him funnier. A legendary speaker, Ira Hayes, had similar effect: he was introduced as an 'ambassador of good will' from National Cash Register Company, walked out looking like the dull, little guy from the corporate back office you never wanted to be stuck next to on a long flight, started out as such then suddenly exploded into a dynamo, running, using flip-pages and goofy props, speaking at gale-force speed, and he was funny – but a helluva lot funnier because of the contrast with your negative anticipation. There was, incidentally, once a person who joined the National Speakers Association and set out to become a top motivational speaker. His name – really – was Chris Boring. Everybody urged him to change his name and he finally, reluctantly went to the license bureau and got his name legally changed. To Robert Boring. (*Bada-boom.*)

Kern's suggestion could apply to print, too. Let's say you're selling a very complex financial proposition via a long letter and it has to include charts and graphs and mind-numbing statistics. You've all seen the little packets of aspirin used as 'grabbers' attached to sales letters, with some version of "I'm here with the cure for your headaches with…"; in this case, you could attach a packet of instant coffee or No-Doz® and say: "This may be the most boring letter anybody's ever sent you – but it is also the most important financial information you will ever discover, so it's worth staying awake for – so I've attached…" Then, of course, the letter needs to be less boring and heavy-going than that attention getting gimmick suggests.

Incidentally, a lot of "grabbers" and "object mail" is at least whimsical if not outright funny, and is used very, very effectively in connection with serious subjects and sophisticated professional services. The little plastic or tin trash can – "since you've been throwing my letters out, I thought I'd send you a trash can…" ….. the giant eraser – "ignoring my warning may be the biggest mistake…" …. the rubber chicken of vaudeville fame…."this is no joke…" and so on. Many fear this depreciates their status as a professional or significance of their message, but their fear is just that, a *fear*. Ad man Donny Deutsch tells of securing an appointment with an auto company CEO by delivering one actual, full-size car part after another to the guy's house with notes attached: to the steering wheel – "we'll steer you in…", to the muffler – "you need to make some noise", etc. Did that risk being written off as an annoying clown? I suppose so, but as the cliché says, even the turtle has to stick his neck out to get anywhere. Where we must always get before we can ever sell anything or persuade anyone of anything is to Attention.

Back to pure self-deprecating humor – illustrated by the cuff-links story. I've heard many speakers tell it and I doubt it's actually happened to them all, but it did actually happen to me, and heck, maybe we're all this dumb. Anyway, here's my version:

"I'm in a very, very small town. Joan Rivers said she visited a town so small they had their annual fashion show at Sears. No models - they just held open the catalog and the clerks would point. The one I found myself stuck in was so small that at their 4th of July town picnic they had a firework show. So I'm stuck here, unpacking, the night before a speaking gig, when I discover I forgot to pack my cuff-links. The little motel had no gift shop. I asked the desk clerk where the town's best clothing store was and she said "The Wal-Mart." I got the cab and raced over to The Wal-Mart, to the jewelry counter - where you can get a 500 KT cubic plastic wedding ring in its very own little zip-loc bag - and found no cuff-links. Down the street, though, the more upscale Target. No luck. Finally K-Mart. By now, I'm pissed off, frustrated, cursing a place so bumpkiny you can't even find one stinking set of cuff-links. I'm stranded in Idiot-ville. In that tone of voice I explain to the clerk in the clothing department at K-Mart that I am a Very Important Person here for a Very Important Speaking Engagement with my French cuff dress shirt and no cuff-links and I must get some and I've been all over the burg hunting some and surely, somewhere in this entire store, they must have one set of cuff-links. "No sir, I'm sorry, we don't", she said, in tone and pace you use patiently speaking to a 4 year old, "but sir, we do have men's dress shirts with button cuffs. You could just buy a shirt, Sir." Yes, I could.

It can then be used to make a point. For example, myopia. How we get focused and mentally locked in on our one way of doing things, the only way we can see to solve a problem. I can go from there to the concept of 'marketing incest' and the need for broader, more diverse exposure to what works in many business – one of the things I sell. Or to the need for 'fresh eyes', to sell consulting, coaching or mastermind groups.

Texas Bix Bender says "if you get to thinkin' you're a powerful and important person try influencin' somebody else's dog." People love hearing about stuffing coming out of a stuffed shirt. Glenn Turner, former NFL head referee Jim Tunney and countless other speakers have used the "Do You Know Who I Am?" story - you know this one. It ends with: the waiter says: "Well, sir, do you know who I am?" "No." "Well, I am the man in charge of the butter." I have my own versions. One involves getting arrested on St. Patrick's Day wearing a green leotard and white sport coat, while driving with a very inebriated, popular local radio personality who was, himself, dyed green. When stopped he confronted the cop with the "do you know who I am?" challenge. The other has me backstage in an old, downtown theater, with Zig Ziglar:

> Our host is very, very, very excited about having us two legendary superstars of stage, screen and speaking in his dusty theater. He's gushing. In comes a volunteer to replenish the coffee, water and day-old Danish. She's maybe 18 years old, with teal and orange and purple hair, a nose ring, and something affixed to one ear vaguely resembling a silver-plated cockroach. He grabs her, brings her to us, and enthusiastically informs her that she is in the presence of two of the most influential people and biggest stars who've ever graced this theater. She looked us

both up and down, and disdainfully mumbled "They sure don't *look* famous" and walked off.

You might think I'd be humbled. You'd be wrong.

If you start thinkin' you're important,
try giving instructions to somebody else's dog.

How To Be A Braggart And Use Self-Deprecating Humor

I've long made a point of describing myself as 'a famous person nobody's heard of'. In explaining this, I get to be mildly self-deprecating, noting that it is safe to go with me to Starbucks without fear of being surrounded by autograph seekers and paparazzi, but I also get to convey the fact that I am famous with people who count; the same entrepreneurs

I'm selling to when telling the story. It lightens the uncomfortable weight of the bragging, but permits the bragging nonetheless. And sometimes you must brag. You need to establish yourself as someone they must pay attention to. For example, I like to tell audiences that I own a lot of racehorses, as short-hand symbol of wealth and success they aspire to; the ability to indulge pricey passions, but I usually work in that I can't be *too* smart since I own investments that eat while I sleep, and with the steeds where I have partners, I seem to own the lame legs. If I talk about flying by private jet, I explain that it's cost justified – because I get free parking. These lines take sting out of the brag but leave the intended message intact: you should pay attention to my advice because I'm living like you'd like to be.

Never lose sight of the fact that it's not just laughter we're after. You have points to make, and you must choose and use humor to make those points.

There is a good, old joke useful as preface to some bit of necessary bragging – whether about your 25th year of marriage (eliciting guaranteed approval from any audience, and utter amazement from some) or about the gigantic yacht you just bought with the spoils from the moneymaking system you're selling. You probably know the joke. It goes like this:

> The elderly Jewish gentleman goes into the Catholic church's confessional, and - in a very, very Yiddish voice - tells the priest he has something he must confess, then proceeds to tell of sitting at the counter at his favorite deli having a late night nosh; in come three young, drop-dead gorgeous, busty blonde triplets

who've been out night-clubbing; they flirt with him; they take him home; and he spends all night in bed with all three of them doing things and having things done to him he'd never even imagined before. The priest says, "Before we discuss the sin, sir, it's obvious from your accent you are Jewish and if you don't mind my asking - why are you telling this to me?" And the gentleman says: "At my age, I'm telling *everybody.*"

Chapter 4

STORIES THAT SAY "IF I CAN DO IT..."

This is one of the most important story categories for most speakers, as most are selling some proposition requiring a change in behavior, development of new skills, acting on some new opportunity, and are confronting the prospect's own self-doubts and poor self-image. The speaker/seller who can somehow convey the "if I can do it, anybody can do it, and have an easier time of it that I did" idea believably has huge advantage.

> *"I have no self-confidence.*
> *When women tell me yes,*
> *I advise them to think it over."*
>
> *- Rodney Dangerfield*

Some people own this. Glenn Turner, for example, has a cleft palate and, as he puts it, "talks funny", and is an 8th grade drop-out, so when he stood on stage flouting his multi-millionaire achievements through selling and said "if I can do it – surely you can..." people found it impossible not to agree. If it's not so obvious, you need to bring it out and make it clear that you did not have some genetic or other advantages they lack, enabling you to do 'x' but barring them from doing so. When I speak to rank beginners and novices about starting their own information marketing businesses, I, of course, make my success known, but I also tell my story of "the cat that licked stamps." You'll find the story as I usually tell it on pages 389-390 of *My Unfinished Business,* the Glazer-Kennedy/ Advantage edition. It tells of my being left with my ex-wife's cat, and it and I getting my mailings out.

There's humor people can identify with in my being left the cat by my departing ex-wife, the cat's irascible personality. There's always laughter from my description of the cat actually licking the stamps – which I demonstrate visually, holding up an imaginary strip of stamps, sticking out my tongue, and slurping from side to side. This is one of the times I wish I had Gene Simmons' tongue. Anyway, it works nicely as a humorous story. It also handily delivers the message that you don't need computers and web sites and lots of other resources or a lot of money to get started. If I got going with little more than a cat that licked stamps, anybody can do this.

This is much more influential than telling a factual story matter of fact. Just saying that I was broke and dumb and started out stuffing my own envelopes on my coffee table every night while watching TV just as anybody still could today is not near as interesting and visual as is the story of the cat that licked stamps.

Creating Pictures In Their Minds

Funny mental pictures are helpful in humorous speaking or writing and in selling. The mental picture of a fat cat sitting there licking stamps is, itself, funny. That's why, for example, when I created Jeff Paul's get-rich-in-mail-order pitch, which has remained in use now for almost 20 years through print ads, direct-mail and TV infomercials, I didn't say: how to make $4,000.00 a day sitting at your kitchen table – I said: how to make $4,000.00 a day sitting at your kitchen table *in your underwear.* Of all the magazines those ads ran in successfully, one magazine insisted the underwear references be taken out. And there the ad failed miserably.

We think mostly in images. We read words or hear words and then instantly translate them into pictures inside our minds. Recently, a client of mine returned to selling by tele-seminars after experimenting for months with webinars that produced much poorer results. He concluded that, in his case, the pictures people were creating in their own minds were more persuasive than the actual things shown during the webinars. I'm an avid collector of and listener to old radio broadcasts, comedies and dramas, and am often more entertained by listening with eyes closed and letting my own imagination make the pictures than I would be watching it as TV program. Try listening to the original *War Of The Worlds* radio broadcast, then watch any version of the movie you like – the radio broadcast is much scarier, because of what you can't see and must picture for yourself. Honest, try it.

Of course, some things funny are best seen. The YouTube video of the little pup stuck on its back unable to get up on its feet is funny – it got over a million views - but is not funny at all unseen and described. On the other hand, I have a true story of working with a time-share company bringing elderly Jewish couples from Manhattan up to the woods, to stay in rustic cabins, and the entire selling operation sabotaged by black bears....Izzy and Goldie opening their cabin door in the morning, cups of coffee in hand, ready to sit on the porch and marvel at the fresh air and birds chirping in the pine trees, and finding a gigantic momma black bear with three cubs parked there....and it is much funnier in the telling than if I showed a video of it.

This is why humorous stories have to be carefully crafted with attention to details put in, details deliberately omitted – you have to think about the picture you want to occur in the listener's or reader's mind, and what you want left to his imagination, what you need to precisely control. Mentioning a "stunning blonde" leaves an enormous amount of flexibility. Describing her as "a stunning blonde, in a too tight, too short dress, teetering on spike heels the height of the Eiffel Tower, wearing diamond earrings the size of Buicks" imposes more control over the picture formed – but still, one person will instantly conjure up someone they know, another recall an ex-wife, another some famous actress. Each listener will pick a different color for the dress, a different hair-style, different jewelry, how short the dress is. And it'll all happen inside their minds in a nanosecond.

The Secret Humorous Story Ingredient That Helps Your Cause More Than Any Other

When you craft and use a humorous story, particularly a self-deprecating or If-I-can-do-it personal story, **what is the objective?** If you know what people really, deep-down want from you (in order to buy from you) answering that question is easy. The reason these stories – as well as self-deprecating humor – are so important to most audiences is that they are looking to you for *encouragement*.

In selling almost anything, you are asking people to envision themselves going from somewhere to somewhere else, often from ignorance, incompetence and anxiety to knowledge, skill and prideful accomplishment. This is true for the guy working at Home Depot, selling to the young couple contemplating painting and wallpapering their own home and fearing a disaster, or me, selling some kind of opportunity from the stage. If the Accomplished-Expert can take them backwards in time to when he was them; with some self-deprecating humorous story or confession be as awkward and clumsy or unsure of self or home decorating, technology, moneymaking or whatever challenged as they fear and feel they are; then flash-forward to Success, he creates confidence for them.

This is why I talk about, personally, mastering the process of going from being terrible at something to great at it, by having done just that so many times with so many things. There is not a single thing that has made me rich or prominent or gives me great satisfaction – including selling, speaking, writing, racing horses – that I didn't start out embarrassingly awful at. People fear their lack of natural talent more than anything else, and believe that others successful at something have talent that they lack. I honestly do not believe I have *any* talent. Not a lick. If I do, at age 54, I haven't yet discovered what it is. I do have some deliberately, highly developed *skills*. And anybody can develop skill. There are, of course, people who quite obviously possess extraordinary talent and for whom accomplishment in something appears to comes easily. Tiger Woods and Michael Jordan leap to mind, although it'd be a mistake to discount how young they started developing skill to match their talent, and how much they worked and work at it. But there are far, far, far, far, far more top achievers in every endeavor who are absent talent, who started out awful, who struggled to get from incompetent to competent – a process anyone can use.

This is a *reassuring* discussion. If it can be told with humor, so much the better. For example, I tell of being on a program as a speaker very early on, and having my performance witnessed by the founder of the National Speakers Association, Cavett Robert. Cavett was the kindest, gentlest, most diplomatic of souls who could always be counted on to find some way to encourage anybody. When I asked him what he thought of my presentation, he slowly said, "With all that you know about advertising and promotion, you need to be careful not to promote yourself too effectively and too aggressively too quickly. All you'll do is speed up the rate at which the world finds out – you're no good."

Ouch.

I was pretty darned awful. And it took some work to replace each aspect of being awful with being good. Ultimately, of course, I became one of the highest income non-celebrity speakers in America for a span of more than a decade, exceeding $1-million a year from speaking, part-time. I was once asked, by a very indignant National Speakers Association member whose name many of you might know, who had little respect for my speaking artistry, what the hell was *I* doing on the #1 seminar tour in America with Zig Ziglar and the panoply of celebrities? I answered that I was making $50,000.00 a day.

> *"I am NOT a failure.*
> *I'm a success that hasn't happened yet.*
> *My credit card company says*
> *they're not canceling my card.*
> *They're just holding it until I happen."*
>
> *- Gene Perret*

Sometimes I do open call-in days for our Glazer-Kennedy Insider's Circle™ Members, when they get 10 or 15 minutes of private conversation with me, ostensibly to ask business questions and get business advice. But 50% of those calls involve them asking me about how I recovered from being broke, how I overcame my booze problem, how I'm coping with diabetes, how I handle pressure, how I get so much done. They talk about failures that haunt and hinder them, spouses who lack faith in them. They look to me for encouragement.

On one such call, a guy who'd built a $10-million dollar a year company from scratch and done over $40-million in business had screwed up, made a series of mistakes, lost everything, had saved nothing, had a wife who'd lost all confidence in him and four kids to feed, and told me that two days ago he'd been heading out to apply for a job driving a bus but read my newsletter over morning coffee and I'd talked him out of giving up on himself and now he was on the phone to hear me tell him, go get 'em buddy, you know how to make money, you did it once, you can do it again – and here's how *I* know; 'cuz *I've* been where you are. Which is exactly what I told him. I told him a funny story about having my car repossessed. And I told him Trump's self-deprecating, humorous story: During the real estate crash, while walking down the street with his wife, Trump pointed to an apparently homeless beggar set up in a doorway selling pencils, and said to her: "See that man? He's worth a billion dollars more than I am." Of course, The Donald tells this better first-person that I just abbreviated. Yes, even Donald Trump can be self-deprecating for purpose.

That's what I do, more than anything else: encourage people.

Don't underestimate this: *everybody's* looking for encouragement. It is a way you can create enormous value out of the "thin air" of your own life experiences and a bit of work at developing humorous stories about them.

"A former girlfriend remembers Bill Gates
as being boring and having bad breath.
He remembers her as not having $100-billion."

– Conan OmBrien

Chapter 5

ATTACK WITH HUMOR

f you must attack another person or entity, the best way to win is by making him or it appear foolish and ridiculous with humor. For politicians, media ridicule is the most dangerous hazard of all. Ask Dan Quayle. Or Sarah Palin, who the media has done its best to Dan Quayle, the verb.

Had I been running against Hillary Clinton in the 2008 primaries, I would have used columnist Mark Shields' line about the unpleasant specter of First Husband Bill wandering the halls of the White House in bathrobe and furry slippers with nothing to do --- heck, he couldn't *behave* when he was running the country from the Oral, uh, Oval Office, so what can we expect from him under *these* circumstances? Then I would have spoken seriously about the choice between going backward to the 1990's, to a co-presidency, to a country and Congress consumed with scandal, to the Lincoln bedroom as a motel for fat cat contributors, for health care policy in secret meetings with insurance lobbyists OR going forward into the 21st century with a new broom to finally sweep Washington clean of the muck of scandal and partisan politics of hatred.

I would plant that Bill in pajamas wandering the halls picture firmly in everybody's minds.

It is the picture planted in the minds that can be most harmful. Think Dukakis driving the tank. Or John Kerry in that silly windsurfing photo, or the sillier hunting shot, in camouflage outfit fresh from the box and neatly pressed. Or the mental picture drawn from his standing at a Philly cheese steak stand and asking if he could please have his with Brie. *Deadly.*

But if I had been Hillary running against Obama in those same primaries, I would have called him that Earnest Young Man – never called him by name – and talked about sending in a child to do a *woman's* job. But I would precede that with a confession, a self-deprecating story about some foolish or embarrassing thing I did as a naïve young person just starting out in politics decades ago. I would say that when I listen to the Earnest Young Man's soaring speeches I get excited, but when I closely examine his naïve ideas – like personally sitting down and negotiating with terrorists – I see my naïve and foolish self of 20 years ago in him and I shudder at the thought of letting a Student Driver leapfrog to the most important and powerful position in the world. And I would finally point out that we just suffered through 8 years with Little Georgie trying to learn on the job; do we want another 8 years of schooling going on at our expense? I'd even have a funny cartoon of Little Georgie and Little Obama in short pants, each reaching up and holding somebody's hand – Georgie to Dick Cheney, Obama to a question mark. And at the end I'd playfully say that it was all meant in good, clean fun; that I thought he could make a very good President *someday* and that I truly admired his *youthful* enthusiasm.

Yes, this would be widely and sharply criticized as vicious, as negative campaigning, even as juvenile. But the images created would stick. The mud would be impossible to wash off. If you have to go after somebody, this is the way to do it. Early in the general campaign, McCain ran a TV commercial linking Obama with Paris Hilton and Britney Spears, making him out to be a "celebrity" of no substance. Paris Hilton, a consummate self-promoter, eagerly agreed to appear in a spoof of the spot made for YouTube by a couple aspiring filmmakers. McCain's spot was more effective than a 'straight' one. It was funny to the faithful, and got more free media airings than a non-funny commercial would have.

Using Humor To Create Differentiation

In my Million Dollar Speech originally crafted for my end of day, clean-up batter position at Peter Lowe's SUCCESS rallies, I was speaking to salespeople and business owners who – for the most part – owned a lot of books and tapes and had just spent 8 hours hearing a lot of stuff they'd already heard 1,000 times before. Quickly I made fun of sales trainers teaching 365 closes; didn't they know one good one that worked? Fake experts who sold only in their memories and ran businesses only in their nightmares. Etc. Without naming any names, I made fun of all the pretenders and delivered the message that I was different and daring and about to say something different and daring. Of course, I could not have come out and just flatly said: *every sales and marketing blabbermouth you've got on tape at home or heard here today is blowing smoke up your ass and I'm here to tell you the truth.* That would have been offensive and arrogant. And I wouldn't even go that far. In fact, I think that Tom Hopkins, Zig Ziglar, Brian Tracy are all well worth listening to. But I *did* want to telegraph differentiation in a powerful yet palatable way. So I did it with humor. Immediately prior to that, I stopped some of the hordes stampeding to the exits in their tracks and brought them back to their seats with humorous reference to the traffic jam they'd suffered that morning and the reality it was waiting for them now – "if you leave now, you're not going anywhere." In that case I was actually attacking a decision they'd made and in the act of carrying out.

Occasionally, I've wanted to position Tony Robbins as less of a celebrity, less credible. On those occasions, I describe him as "the guy with the big head and big teeth you see in late night TV infomercials" and do not say his name. While I haven't actually said anything bad about him, I have diminished him, with humor. People chuckle at the description. It seems good-natured. McCain did this just once during a presidential debate, referring to Obama as "that guy over there" – and got laughs. Unfortunately, McCain lacked the testicles or intelligence to keep at it and continuously diminish his opponent.

Three Types of Dragons You Can Slay With Humor

The characterizing of an opponent with a humorous identity can be a very powerful thing. My suggestion for Hillary of characterizing Obama as The Earnest Young Man; my characterizing of the other experts as sales trainers who sell only in their memories – if you develop such a description for your opponent and stick with it, you can win the battle of positioning. Spiro Agnew got some traction for a while, referring to the media constantly as the Nattering Nabobs Of Negativity. For many years, I've made much of Big, Dumb Companies, pointing out that the bigger they are, the dumber they are. This resonates with my audiences of small business owners and independent entrepreneurs; they *like* believing that the big companies competing with them and usually, actually besting them are stupid, lumbering behemoths.

If you've read the book or seen the play *Wicked* – which I highly recommend – you know there's a bit more to that witch thing than was told in the original *Wizard of Oz*. But really, once you're stuck with the label 'Wicked Witch of the West', what are you going to do to change peoples' minds? It's a rather confining identity, don't you think?

Of course, you may think you have no opponent or enemy to attack. But you're wrong. Everybody selling anything squares off against some competitive alternative, even if that's the buyer doing nothing. That opponent can be and usually should be demonized. If I was in the business of selling big, gas-guzzling SUV's right now, I'd run ads showing big guys crumpling themselves into balls to squeeze into the miniature "green" cars....no place to even put a briefcase, so it has to be put in a little trailer towed behind....people standing around laughing at the spectacle. I'd show the commercial for the little car that has the hamsters driving it and mock it. I'd make giving up your full-size, man-sized car the equivalent of putting on a frilly pink apron and helping ice the cupcakes in the kitchen while your buddies are next door watching the game on a big screen. Apple has been doing this for at least a year, very effectively, with its TV commercials featuring the cool guy as the Mac; the nerdy, bookish, constantly scheming loser as the PC. By the way, in case you hadn't realized it, those commercials are the old Road Runner and Coyote cartoons re-cycled.

Furthermore, if you don't think you have an enemy, your customers most certainly do have one. Every group has somebody they fear or hate or oppose. To sell to a group, you want to be clearly positioned as on their side, sympathetic to if not actually engaged in their battle against their evil foe. For salespeople in a big organization, this might be the idiots in the ivory tower at the corporate headquarters. For chiropractors, it can be the arrogant, egotistical M.D.'s who look down their noses at D.C.'s. *What's the difference between God and an M.D.? God doesn't think he's an M.D.* That's a joke template, by the way. *What's the difference between God and Obama? God doesn't think he's Obama. Obama gets better press.* Anyway, every group has an enemy that you can gain points by attacking, and can best attack with disdainful and sarcastic humor.

Like him or hate him, you should – from a business standpoint – acknowledge that Rush Limbaugh has built and sustained the largest radio listenership ever, has a fiercely loyal audience, and has made himself very, very, very rich by doing so. One of the most reliable, most frequently used tools in his toolbox: comedic characterizations of his and his audience's enemies. Femin-nazis. Tree-huggers. Senator Harry Reid as Dingy Harry. Even, most dangerously, the *Obama, The Magic Negro* song he has played. Take note. Rush knows what he's doing.

Incidentally, liberal film-maker, author and professional gadfly Michael Moore has made a fortune for himself with attack humor too, specializing in 'stunts' and ambush interviews designed to make his targets look foolish. Bill Maher tried following in Moore's footsteps with his movie attacking religion in the same way, but Moore's success eluded him. Maher's movie left the theaters almost overnight. Surprising to many, given that Bill has an audience and a platform centered around his own show on HBO. What did he miss? There aren't that many atheists. There's a large constituency on the left happy to have someone like Moore attack and mock auto companies, insurance companies or capitalism itself; a large constituency on the right happy to have someone like Rush Limbaugh attack militant feminists or environmentalists or liberals. There's no large constituency eager to have somebody act as their surrogate in attacking Christianity. Even those non-practicing or agnostic, have fathers and mothers and other family members who are believers, and they, themselves, are not really *avowed* non-believers. At least not late at night, alone, in the dark. Also, religion poses no threat to them. They may not believe in it but they don't view it as an enemy. Maher picked the wrong target. Moore has picked the right ones, and each time, timely ones. (By the way, you can read my 'Michael Moore Is A Big, Fat Idiot' essay, Chapter 76, in my book *My Unfinished Business.*)

One final way to use humorous, sarcastic, negative characterizations in selling is against the non-buyers. Top copywriter John Carlton makes the point that your sales copy must be incredibly strong, in order to move the giant somnambulant sloth (picture Michael Moore) off the couch and to the phone. It's a demeaning image I've borrowed to describe the majority of people too slothful and lazy to buy, thus challenging you: are you a big, fat, lazy somnambulant sloth like so many, or are you a person of rare initiative, ambition, a person of action? I talk about the Mediocre Majority and how they act. I create a humorous but very unflattering description of a Loser, and then dare my prospect to identify himself as a member of that Loser's tribe – by not buying, of course.

There are endless variations. Arnold Schwarzenegger characterized those not embracing his ideas for physical fitness as weak and flabby "girly-men" – a charge he also leveled against the California state legislature while

Governor. Walt Disney talked about "lawn mowers" and "courageous creatives"; the "lawn mower" the guy with no imagination, no spark, who could have his hands put on the handle of the mower and would then just plod endlessly along, following the mower up, down, up, down, up down, until the entire lawn was mowed and then just continue again from the original starting place, forever plodding, eyes downward, shoulders hunched, getting nowhere. Zig characterizes the majority of people as having "stinkin' thinkin'" – and obviously, you don't want *that*, do you?

He has stinkin' thinking.

Yes, gentle, kind, benevolent, Christian Zig uses "division politics" and "negative characterization" to sell. How 'bout that? This is all about the power-principle of **Divide And Conquer.** You divide your audience or prospects into two groups; one, sad, pathetic, foolish, lazy, even "stinky"; the other the bright, admirable, cool group. The reader, listener, prospect must then decide for himself which he is, by the action he takes or fails to take, that you've put before him. It's best to do this with humor. Not only doesn't your prospect want to be in the un-cool group, he damned sure doesn't want to be in the un-cool group *being made fun of.*

If saddled with a monologue he thought weak, Johnny Carson would open by making fun of the terrible audience they'd had the night before. He would humorously describe them, making it clear they were too dumb to get the jokes. This set up that night's audience to laugh at everything riotously, to avoid being as bad as the prior night's bunch of dim bulbs. Letterman, a Carson student and protégé, occasionally uses the same tactic.

In closing sales, I've often described the folks who live in Think-It-Over, Iowa, where the only traffic light stays yellow, the only color is gray, there's only one item on the restaurant's menu, and nothing ever changes – every family's TV stays on whatever channel it's set on when first delivered to the home, because changing it requires decision, which they must think over and never stop thinking it over until they die. This is my attack on procrastination. I tell the audience that those who are happy living like Think-It-Over Iowans should definitely not take my resources home. They'll find them deeply disturbing and unsettling. It would be best if they just stayed comfortably in their seats, while those who abhor dull sameness and like courageously challenging the status quo and are decisive individuals go to the tables at the back of the room...

I used to use that bit a lot. I haven't much, in a number of years – mostly because I haven't been selling from the stage in tough enough environments where I felt such heavy handedness warranted, and heavy handed it is, although think about how much more ugly it would be stripped of the humorous, fictional town and just said straight up. The humor of it is *lubricant*.

Fictional places, incidentally, are staples of humor and humorous storytelling. Think of Dr. Seuss, Garrison Keillor and Lake Wobegon – where *all* the children are above average. Of course, real places have humorous identities, too. California is widely regarded as an insane asylum with palm trees and highways. Given that Jerry 'Moonbeam' Brown is talking about again running for Governor there, the reputation is reinforced. The deep South is viewed as home of shoeless, toothless hicks who live in trailer parks. Jeff Foxworthy's 'You Might Be A Redneck' comedy, good-natured as it is, reinforces that stereotype. New Jersey: dead bodies in the water, garbage on the shore. The opening of The Sopranos. The anti-New Jersey jokes told by the Governor of New York character on SNL's Weekend Up-Date. Alaska: moose wandering around. Florida: old people driving 4 miles per hour en-route to the early bird buffet. London, England: bad teeth, bad food, bad weather. I was there. The weather was fine. Australia: Kangaroos. Crocodile Dundee. Such stereotype identities are useful as foundation for humor and, if you choose, dividing and diminishing people. Making fun of the kooks in California plays well in the Midwest. Making fun of the dimwits in the Midwest's small towns clinging to their guns 'n Bibles plays well in San Francisco – ask Obama; he used it at a fundraising dinner speech there. By making fun of Others in Other Places, you identify the ones you are speaking to in their place in which you've arrived as the smart ones or ones with better values and morals or otherwise superior ones. Any way to divide and conquer can work to your advantage in selling, and any way to do so can be enhanced with humor.

"Dear Mr. Insert-Name: I am writing to alert you
to the fact that some moron has apparently
stolen sheets of your letterhead and
is writing stupid, insipid, embarrassingly foolish letters
to important and successful people like me. I've enclosed
the ridiculous one I received in hope it will assist you
in tracking down this deranged person
before he does further damage to your reputation,
hanging by a thread as it is…"

  - Based on Dr. Charlie Jarvisms response to a complaint letter

---

Chapter 6

THE F-BOMB, DIRTY JOKES AND STEPPING IN IT ON STAGE

WARNING: this Chapter contains adult language some may judge profane or find offensive. You can skip it. Jump right over to Page 83. And please don't send me some fucking letter complaining about it. You were warned.

ill Cosby correctly says it is much more difficult to 'work clean.' That's why the majority of comedians work dirty. Some *very* dirty. Dennis O'Leary, for example. Even people with a mainstream reputation as 'nice', like Bob Saget, the Dad in the TV sitcom, when appearing as a stand-up comic, is filthy. And almost all bad comedians and lazy comedians work dirty.

Working clean *is* a handicap. First of all, it rules out 90% of the truly dirty jokes, and many of them are very funny. Some can be cleaned up and made to still be funny. But most can't. Second, there are any number of jokes that are a lot funnier with a strategically placed F word than without it. The Sherlock Holmes/Dr. Watson camping story I use gets much bigger laughs with 'somebody stole our *fucking* tent ' than with 'somebody stole our tent.' This is why most of the top stand-up comics to come and go over the last 30 years have 'worked dirty'. However. Those who transcended stand-up and became comedic icons and bigger-than-comedy personalities – Cosby, Newhart, Berman, more, and I suppose you could include Seinfeld, Foxworthy – learned to work clean. Privately, I'm sure they enjoy telling filthy jokes as much as any comic. But they made a strategic, difficult choice with their acts.

You **have little choice**. It would be rare for anybody reading this book to have opportunities to work dirty, and there is no middle ground. Saying the F word once in two hours is once too many in most seminar, business speaking and platform selling environments. Even if that environment happens to be made up of all male salesmen it's riskier than it's worth. Believe it or not there are sensitive guys out there. Just as example, our 2008 SuperConference featured Gene Simmons and the several pages in our brochure included the two Playboy covers, one featuring Gene's long-time girlfriend Shannon Tweed; the other, Gene surrounded by naked women wearing KISS make-up. Each cover about the size of two thumbs. The nudity partial. We had *a guy* complain that it was demeaning to women and offensive. Oprah'd be *so* proud. Of course, we can afford not to care about him or the tiny contingent within our large member base that he might represent – and we don't. But in a closed room, on stage, facing an audience, you may not want to risk even one swash of blue.

I'm pretty coarse in private, and have to work at editing what's about to come out of my mouth, especially when on stage for hours or even days, with audiences I have familiarity and on-going relationship with. There's temptation to "let loose" a little, and to use some "blue" comedy, and in very recent years, in certain controlled and very friendly environments, I've experimented a little, and very occasionally, had an accident. But I can afford this luxury. You probably can't.

Kathy Griffin, the comic actress of 'The D-List', took us – in her reality show – behind the scenes to a corporate gig she had for a hair products company's sales convention, in Las Vegas. You might think somebody hiring Kathy would reasonably expect F-bombs dropping like it was Hiroshima, and she might think that she'd have that freedom. But they put her on first thing Sunday morning – not a good time for any comedy. She came rolling out to the half asleep, half hungover Vegas audience and yelled "What the *fuck* are we doing here at 8:00 IN THE MORNING?" You may not feel it in print, but screamed, this does work much, much better with the fuck in it than out. (That's why it's virtually impossible to use any hunk of Sam Kinison's rants, F-neutered.) But this group was mysteriously unprepared for her, they were straight-laced corporate types, the timing was terrible, and she might as well have been in front of Baptist preachers. It zoomed downhill from there, to a fiery crash. And you can rest assured, she'll never work in that 'town' again.

When Tony Robbins briefly appeared on the Peter Lowe SUCCESS tour – he, there, a Titanic disaster exactly as I'd predicted – his contract specified not using the F word. He was in breach within 30 minutes. And he regularly and casually uses it and other profanity on stage and you might argue that it hasn't hurt him. However, without the singular power of TV celebrity manufactured for him by Guthy-Renker, he'd have found a less tolerant world. And a career is a marathon, not a sprint. Something everybody needs to keep in mind.

You have to understand that **small things leave indelible imprint**. Even the incidental use of profanity or the telling of a dirty joke can overshadow everything else. The shortcut it offers to cheap laughs, the convenience of using a wealth of funny material it provides and the freedom from the discipline of not doing it combine as still poor value balanced against what may be lost in achieving your overriding objectives from speaking to sell or your reputation in the marketplace in general. There's too much too easily lost, too little to be gained.

As an aside, it's worth noting **there are other profanities *unique to certain groups*.** The first time Sydney Biddle Barrows spoke at one of our SuperConferences, she basically told her 'Mayflower Madam' story and gave an insider's peek at the upscale (and illegal) 'escort service' – from which there are so many business insights to be gained her original tell-all book was named a "best business book" by *FORTUNE,* and immediately following the crash of her escort business, she was snapped up to tour and speak to all the YPO groups. (Young Presidents' Organization). In the course of about 90 minutes, she innocently used the *clinical* term "blow job" once, just once. For which we heard *a few* complaints. But toward end she casually mentioned that, among other things, she now had a day job – a prestigious one, as right hand diva to a top hedge fund manager.

Now *this* was, to our group of die-hard entrepreneurs, *real* profanity, and we got *a lot of* grief about it, and for many, it discredited everything in the prior 80 minutes.

I've spoken to chiropractors and dentists for 25 years. Saying anything positive about M.D.'s or somehow linking M.D.'s and D.C.'s is profanity far more vile to them than saying fuck. In fact, you'll easily be forgiven saying 'those fucking M.D.'s'. Saying 'doctors and dentists' is profanity to dentists; it suggests they are lesser; they *are* doctors.

So you can, quite easily and innocently, step in shit without ever uttering any of those words on the George Carlin words-you-can't-say-on-TV or your mom's wash-out-your-mouth-with-soap list.

Oops, There Goes The Audience!

The main areas of high risk – other than dropping the F bomb or using other profanity – are religion, ethnicity, and ill health and death.

People take *their* God pretty seriously.

You can do jokes about your own religion, if they're good-natured, and you're careful. But it's high risk doing jokes about other peoples' religions. I was raised Lutheran, which is basically Catholic without confession. Basically, a bunch of Catholics got pissed off about something, left and started their own thing, kind of Catholic-Lite. The whole thing left a lot of folks confused. We ate fish on Friday, even though it was a Catholic thing, but most Lutherans were still a little nervous that tossing something of that much importance to God overboard, pardon the pun, might not be a smart thing to do. My memory of it all is a little fuzzy, but I think we added a commandment or two just to get a leg up on the Catholics.

RELIGIONS AS CLIFF'S NOTES,

FOR THE TIME-PRESSED....

Taoism	Shit happens.
Hinduism	This shit happened before.
Buddhism	This is only the illusion of shit happening.
Zen	What is the sound of shit happening?
Islam	If shit happens, it is the will of Allah – and it should rain down upon the infidels!
Jehovah's Witnesses	Knock, knock. Who's there? Shit happens.
Protestantism	Shit won't happen if I work harder.
Catholicism	If shit happens, I deserve it. I need to confess.
Judaism	Why does shit always happen to me? Are we a cursed people? Why? I need to atone.
Televangelism	Send money or shit *will* happen *to you*.
Rastafarianism	Smoke that shit!

Jewish comics make a lot of fun of being Jewish, but it's my experience they are pretty humorless when a non-Jew does. Very sensitive. Might have something to do with there always being some dictator somewhere threatening to exterminate them and wipe them off the earth. I imagine it makes you touchy. I was on several Success events with Benjamin Netanyahu, and he didn't seem to have much of a sense of humor about anything. Woody Allen once said that "everybody's a damn anti-Semite. Even I am sometimes and I'm Jewish." Woody Allen said it. Not me. Woody Allen. I've had quite a few Mormon friends and business acquaintances over years, and they're a little touchy about that magic underwear thing, and about polygamy. The few I asked have not found the HBO dark-comedy 'Big Love' funny. Firefighters love 'Rescue Me' though. Go figure. But the bunch least tolerant of their religion being made fun of seem to be the Baptists. Rigid, very rigid.

This is kind of funny – for about ten years I used a little throwaway line I stole outright from Charlie Jarvis, about knowing it was a recession because all the Avon ladies and Jehovah's Witnesses were car-pooling. I expected but never got a complaint from a Jehovah's Witness. But I finally got a very, very virulent complaint from an Avon sales manager.

Anyway, it's hard to imagine much reason for the speaker who speaks to sell to ever have good reason for trying to convert religion into comedy. If you feel compelled, though, as some sort of bonding device with the audience, your model ought to be Garrison Keillor and the way he talks about Episcopalians.

Then there's serious illness and death.

> *"My cousin just died.*
> *He was only 19.*
> *He got stung by a bee*
> *– (pause) –*

> *the natural enemy of*
> *a tightrope walker."*
>
> *- Emo Phillips*

There's a female comedian out on the comedy club circuit now, I'm sorry but I forget her name, and she's a cancer survivor and does her entire routine about cancer. I've seen her work. She's highly skilled and the material is very well-written. But it's still tough on audiences. Too uncomfortable. And the risk about any illness, disability or death joke is that somebody in the audience has just been diagnosed with it or has had a family member die from it. Obama got a lot of flak for an unscripted, off-hand remark about Special Olympics kids made during one of his appearances on *The Tonight Show,* and I thought it was a 'nothing' that didn't deserve any firestorm of criticism, but it shows you how even a hugely popular person can get into a lot of trouble stepping into this territory.

My circus midget story has a rather violent death in it, and I do see people react squeamishly to it. Even though there's no possibility of personal connection; the likelihood of somebody in the audience having lost a loved one to death by hippopotamus is slim.

> *"I stayed up one night*
> *playing poker with Tarot cards.*
> *I got a full house*
> *and four people died."*
>
> *- Steven Wright*

At the Success events, Olympian Mary Lou Retton had bad luck. Twice, maybe even three times during her speeches somebody in the audience popped up and keeled over with heart attacks. On one such occasion, **I turned to Zig and said, "This isn't good. I don't know any good death jokes."** I think that's funny, and you don't often get a chance to use it. He was horrified. I decided – reluctantly – not to use it when I went on stage after her.

"This is what he would have wanted—he was a total neat freak."

There is also the matter of dead heroes. In the 1960's there was a hugely successful comedian, Vaughan Meader, whose entire career was built on his, pardon the term, dead-on impression of John F. Kennedy and his record albums with the entire Kennedy family imitated and mocked. He as Jack, talking to Jackie and Lil' John, created roll on the floor hilarious bits. The albums sold millions of copies and everybody had 'em. My parents played them when friends came over who hadn't heard them and everybody gathered around the record player and laughed like hell. Meader's career ended when JFK's life did. To my knowledge, Meader never worked in show biz again. And for a long, long, long time, nobody dared do a JFK joke. It's still very risky. Sam Kinison did a bit about schtupping Marilyn on the desk in the Oval Office, but then he was Sam Kinison. Kennedy jokes are not well received at all by anybody. Reagan jokes are not well received by Republicans and other honorable people, but at a cook-out at Barbara Streisand's house, they *kill*.

Illness, dying, death or the dead, all sources of comedy material you probably want to avoid.

Next, gender. You can pretty much tell any nasty, demeaning, vicious joke about men you can think of, whether you are a man or a woman, and especially if you are a woman. But you'd better be very, very careful telling jokes about women, especially if you are a man. Very good-natured, gentle joking about relationships, about the 'men are from Mars and women from Venus' stuff, that a guy can get away with. But if you do the woman-bashing version of a Rosanne Barr men-are-morons routine and women hear it or even find out about it, they'll put a curse on you. One of my all-time favorite cartoons has a befuddled guy standing at the customer service counter of The Feminist Bookstore being told by the clerk: "We DON'T HAVE a humor section."

Ethnicity used to be just fine. I grew up on Polish jokes and Italian jokes. In the 40's and 50's, Pat 'n Mike jokes about the Irish were commonplace. How many men do you need for an Irish funeral? *Six pallbearers and a bartender.* Why did God invent booze? *To keep the Irish from taking over the world.* And, of course, blacks, Mexicans and Asians were all brunt of jokes, ranging from good-natured to vicious. What do you get when you cross a Mexican and an Oriental? *A car thief who can't drive.* Yes, these were told on radio and TV. With no repercussions.

Obviously, those days are long, long gone, and I suppose they should be.

Today, the rules are wobbly. On *Mind Of Mencia* on the Comedy Channel, he tells vicious jokes and does stereotype-based skits derogatory to his own ethnic group, Mexicans, as well as every other group. But Imus hit the Daily Double, with "knappy headed ho's". Blacks, women. Bye-bye career, into exile. Damn few friends, all of a sudden. Of course, the *Reverend* Jesse Jackson wasn't joking when he said, quote, that he wanted to cut off Barack Obama's nuts, but had that been, say, Don Imus or Rush Limbaugh saying it, gelding would seem tame. Chris Rock can attack blacks, separately black women, and separately black men and in doing so, freely use the N word. But that is because he is Chris Rock. Bottom-line is, these rules are too complicated and arbitrary and shifting to navigate. Best just to leave it all alone.

Chapter 7

HOW TO CHEAT AT COMEDY— AND GET AWAY WITH IT

This is probably THE most valuable Chapter in the **book** for 'amateurs', particularly for those who aren't at all gifted at being funny, but still see the value of bringing humor into their speeches, group sales presentations, and sales copy. This Chapter is all about cheating – getting laughs without developing a great deal of skill at doing it. And I don't mean that disrespectfully or snidely. If you're going to develop a lot of comedy skill, it's going to take time, study, dedication, practice and did I mention, time. Not very useful if you have a presentation coming up next week. Or if you just need to deliver presentations now and then, and you aren't deeply interested in being a student of comedy.

An analogy is magic. There are lots of pre-fab magic tricks in a box. Since I'm all thumbs, I've found most of them too hard. But recently even I got my hands on a pre-fab magic trick that I can easily and successfully do, and amaze my victims with it. It's easier to use comedy tricks in a box. Sleight of hand isn't required. So, in this Chapter, I'll give you a big box of comedy tricks anybody can use.

> *"One good aspect of being mediocre is*
> *that you're always at the top of your game."*
>
> *- Kinky Friedman*

It's not easy for stand-up comics to cheat. Carrot Top has done it very successfully, relying entirely on prop comedy. Jonathan, a comedy magician, cheats with malfunctioning magic tricks. Leno cheats a lot, not because he can't deliver jokes in a monologue; he obviously can, but his show requires a lot of content. Filling all that time requires cheating. And there's a lot to be learned – quickly and easily – by watching Leno cheat. And man, oh man, is he cheating a lot. Photos of celebrities who look like their pets. *Eight minutes* of it at a time. An electric race car different celebrities drive around an obstacle course while he talks to them. Cheat, cheat, cheat. Watch and learn. But, by and large, successful stand-up comics are barred from cheating and required to rely on themselves, their scripted routines, and their ability to perform. They are out there naked.

Speakers operating in friendlier, less demanding environments have much greater opportunity to cheat. In speeches to promote your business, seminars and workshops, tele-seminars and webinars, you work in environments wonderfully accepting of cheating at comedy and getting away with it. Same with media: sales letters, brochures, web sites.

As I said, Leno cheats a lot. Once a week, he cheats with funny headlines collected from newspapers and magazines. Any speaker could swipe this bit. He frequently cheats with comical book titles, products and inventions that fail, and other gimmicks. Letterman cheats with his Top Ten List. These are the kinds of cheats you can integrate into speeches and seminars to provide relevant comedy relief that does not require you to be a skilled comedian.

You can cheat with:

- Props
- Funny 'mistakes' – headlines, advertisements
- Lists
- Cartoons
- Short videos
- Jokes Re-Made

Props

Carrot Top's entire comedy routine is based on props; funny items he's manufactured, that he pulls out of a big trunk, quickly jokes about and tosses aside. He is not the first to rely on props. Steve Martin actually made his chops using and mocking tired comedy props like the arrow through the head cap and the iconic rubber chicken. And, there have been and are a lot of speakers who rely on them to various extents. Ira Hayes, who was a top, in demand, famous motivational speaker for three decades – giving a speech titled *Keeping Pace With Tomorrow* (unchanged for those 30 some-odd years!) – had tables of props spanning the stage, and referred to one after the other. I recall the Davy Crockett coonskin cap. If you can find Ira's presentation on video, you should study it. Mike Vance, one of the very best storytelling speakers – both funny and poignant stories – similarly lines up a row of what he calls 'artifacts' to pick up, show and talk about. Other speakers use props much more sparingly. Zig Ziglar is famous for his giant pump brought on stage, and vigorously pumped. Jim Rohn used a chalkboard, switched to a whiteboard only in recent years, as a prop more than a legitimate visual aid.

Props in and of themselves can be funny, even in the hands of relatively unskilled performers. Carrot Top's kind of props are great examples of this. Where might you look for props to suit your purposes? Ad specialty companies. Companies like 3-D Mail Results (www.3DMailResults.com) and Oriental Trading Company (www.OrientalTrading.com), dollar stores, toy stores, novelty shops like Spencer Gifts, magic shops. There's a great prop company called Great Big Stuff (www.GreatBigStuff.com) offering giant-sized pencils, crayons, clocks and many other objects. You can pull up the right prop and let it get laughs for you.

Funny Mistakes

Leno's HEADLINES bit is this. The kind of stupid criminal stories I collect and use are this. Odd products packaged or labeled strangely, commonly found in dollar stores, are this. A book like *The 776 Stupidest Things Ever Said* by Ross and Katryn Petras – one of a series available from any bookseller – are collections of these, easily swiped from. The book *I'm So Sorry: Stories Behind 101 Very Public Apologies* by James Dickerson is a collection of public figures' embarrassments. Celebrity mug shots are readily available online to match some of them. And new ones materialize daily. Years ago, when I did a presentation strictly on advertising, I borrowed from *MAD Magazine's* long-running series of "ads we'd like to see", took current ads and re-did them as "ads that should never have happened" and peppered them throughout my speech, getting cheap laughs every few minutes. Incidentally, there is a book: *MADvertising: A MAD Look at 50 Years of Madison Avenue*, a great collection of all the best satires of advertising that appeared in *MAD Magazine*.

'Stupid criminals' stories are funny mistakes. I collect these stories and use them. Audiences like 'em, and they are done for you. There are even *famous* stupid criminals. Long before he was a country-western star, Merle Haggard was an honest-to-gum outlaw. At age 20, he and some buddies decided to rob a restaurant. They got drunk and waited until 3:00 in the morning, when the joint was sure to be empty. When they broke in through a locked side door, they were shocked to find it full of customers, at 9:00 P.M. Somebody should have stolen a watch. Put Haggard in San Quentin, where he saw Johnny Cash perform – and that's what inspired him to pick up a guitar in the first place. Which, if you wanted to stretch this to making a point, is the classic Zen monk story: the young boy in the village is given a horse as a 16th birthday gift by a traveler and all the villagers are happy for him. The Zen monk says: we'll see. The boy falls from his horse and breaks his back and all the villagers are sad for him. The Zen monk says: we'll see.

A war erupts and all the young men go off to war – except the boy with the broken back, and all the villagers say he was oddly lucky. The Zen master says: we'll see. Merle Haggard can't tell time and his bungled burglary puts him in prison, and his friends and family say he's ruined his life, and the Zen monk says: we'll see. Points? Over-reacting or prematurely, negatively reacting to any business or life event isn't smart. Or my stated principle: nothing is ever as bad or good as it first appears. Of course, if the only point you want to make is that people rise to incredible heights of stupidity, you just string together a series of funny stupid criminal escapades.

Lists

Letterman's nightly TOP TEN LIST is this. It gives you a ready-made framework to come up with pointed humor for your subject, business, product or service – The Top Ten Ways To _____ - or – NOT To _____. The "Religions As Cliff's Notes" on Page 76 is, obviously, a list. With a little research, a list of the ten worst advertising or marketing or business or investing decisions ever made; the ten worst names for restaurants.

There's a list I created and have used for many clients' sales letters for seminars and for opportunities: *How To Get Rich – Instead Of This Opportunity*. The list includes:

> 1: Be born to rich parents. Probably too late for that. Could you still get yourself adopted?
>
> 2: Marry rich. Double-check, maybe your spouse is holding out on you.

3: Hit the lottery. Sure, it's more likely you'll be hit twice by lightning while indoors, but what the heck, you can still hope, right?

4: Invent the next Post-It Note®. Warning: that cool idea you have for a recliner with a beer refrigerator and toilet built in has already been patented.

This list sneers at and mocks peoples' fantasies about getting rich, but humorously enough that people don't take offense.

There's the ever-popular list of book titles, like *Tweet And Grow Rich, The 4-Hour Work Week* and *How To Buy Real Estate With Nothing Down And A Gun*. George Carlin used lists of book titles throughout his career.

Cartoons & Photos

Could there be an easier way to cheat? You can find relevant cartoons from sources that license them – like *The New York Times'* Cartoon Bank, or invest in having custom cartoons created for you, by pros like Vince Palko. You can even make your own if you aren't entirely computer deficient – my Mac has a program called Comic Life right inside. Of course, if you are humor challenged to start with, the idea of coming up with your own cartoons sounds daunting. But many jokes can be converted to cartoons. And collections of Peanuts®, Calvin And Hobbs®, Dilbert®, etc. are available at bookstores, providing gigantic 'swipe files' for inspiration. Online talent brokerages like E-Lance can give you the actual cartoonist, presuming your drawing ability is limited to a smiley-face. For speakers, there are even collections of business-related cartoons available on CD's from companies like Trainer's Warehouse. (www.trainerswarehouse.com)

The cartoons I had Vince Palko do for my *NO B.S. RUTHLESS MANAGEMENT* book, I wrote myself, cribbing ideas from a couple business joke books, and tweaking them to be my own (and avoid outright copyright infringement). If you speak, you probably have your own, original "lines" that lend themselves to cartoons, too. Even dry, straight material can be converted to humor through a cartoon. The "activity/accomplishment" cartoon comes right from un-humorous time management 101 content.

Copyright © Dan Kennedy 2007   Vincent Palko   www.AdToons.com

Humorous or iconic photos are readily available, online from Bettman Archives, or from stock photo companies. All you need to do is talk over it or write your own captions for them. Conversely, if you have a funny idea to communicate, you can search for the perfectly matched photo. Go to a greeting card store and you'll find entire collections of funny cards and postcards that have been created exactly this way. In fact, you may find a photo-with-funny-caption greeting card that will work for you as-is.

Short Videos

Again, the easiest way ever to cheat. These days, YouTube® has provided ready access to thousands of funny videos in just about every category, that you can relate to your subject – even if it's a stretch, and get laughs, and laugh right along with your audience. Obviously, you can easily make your own these days too.

Technically, copyrighted films, TV shows, and cartoons can't be shown in any commercial venues – seminars included – without licensing the rights or at least securing permissions. As a practical matter, speakers use such clips with impunity. I can't advise doing that, but I can point out that, with virtually every movie and TV series on DVD, finding quick clips a few minutes in length that illustrate your points and are laugh-out-loud funny, and integrating them right into your Power-Points presentation (if you insist on using that thing) or otherwise popping them on throughout your presentation is as easy as pie. I recently bought a package of DVD's with six hours of classic TV commercials from the 50's, 60's and 70's – *Don't Touch That Dial!* – which I think I paid about $20 for. Betcha I can find some that'll get laughs, that I can use during a presentation.

A great way to use video clips to cheat is to use funny or familiar video absent its sound-track, while you talk over it. *Beverly Hillbillies* footage behind you while you say something profound about getting rich, for example, would be a quick 'n dirty way for you to be funny – even if you aren't.

Jokes Re-Made

This requires more skill and work than any of the other cheats I've mentioned here. But it is something I've done a great deal of personally, so it'd be unfair not to include it. Taking a joke out of a joke book and just telling it is something I don't recommend. Most sound like just that, a stock, off the shelf joke. And most people aren't sufficiently skilled to deliver them well. But there are tons of jokes nicely gathered up for you in joke books. I like to find one that can be "massaged" into a personal story. So, here are two jokes right out of a joke book:

He met a friend he hadn't seen for years and asked him how he was feeling. "Awful," replied the friend. "On top of my high blood pressure, I've got arthritis and diabetes." "Sorry to hear that - what about your business?" And the friend says, "Oh, that's doing fine, Same business I've always been in - health food stores."

Second joke: A woman who had just learned that fish is brain food, told her doctor about it and asked how much fish she should eat daily to improve her mind. "In your case, it's not necessary to eat much," her doctor said. "Just take for breakfast every morning a baby whale on toast."

Here they are, fixed for me:

As you know, I do a lot of work in the health, diet and nutrition fields, as a marketing consultant and advertising copywriter, print ads, direct-mail campaigns, even TV infomercials - so I'm always paying attention to the latest trends and fads and products. The other day a friend who knows about my work told me she'd watched an infomercial about how great fish oil was for improving brain and memory function the night before an appointment at her doctor's, so she asked him how much seafood she needed to eat every day to improve her mind. He told her not much - he suggested every morning for breakfast having a *baby whale on toast.* Apparently sarcasm's a free bonus at his office. I don't know about this health thing. We all battle it. Recently I ran into a business acquaintance I hadn't seen in years and I asked him how he was feeling. "Awful," he said. "On top of my high blood pressure, I've got arthritis and diabetes now." "Sorry to hear that - what about your business?" And he says, "Oh, that's doing fine. Same business I've always been in - *health food.*"

Now look at it again, by the numbers.... (1): I put a one sentence set-up for me in front of the jokes. (It happens to be a self-promotional sentence too, that might bring forward a client.) (2): In the first of the jokes I used, I stuck in reference to an infomercial, which modernizes the old joke, and ties it to my work again. (3): I also switched "fish" to "fish oil," a modernizing touch. (4): To be sure the audience gets the 'whale line', I'd deliver it in a sarcastic tone, but I also added the line about it being sarcasm. Taking nothing for granted. (5): I built a tiny bridge from one joke to the next. (6): I used the second joke nearly as-was, alternating only the business from health food stores to health food

(1): As you know, I do a lot of work in the health, diet and nutrition fields, as a marketing consultant and advertising copywriter, print ads, direct-mail campaigns, even TV infomercials - so I'm always paying attention to the latest trends and fads and products. The other day a friend who knows about my work told me (2): she'd watched an infomercial about how great (3): fish oil was for improving brain and memory function the night before an appointment at her doctor's, so she asked him how much seafood she needed to eat every day to improve her mind. He told her not much - he suggested every morning for breakfast having a *baby whale on toast.* (4): Apparently sarcasm's a free bonus at his office. (5): I don't know about this health thing. We all battle it. (6): Recently I ran into a business acquaintance I hadn't seen in years and I asked him how he was feeling. "Awful," he said. "On top of my high blood pressure, I've got arthritis and diabetes now." "Sorry to hear that - what about your business?" And he says, "Oh, that's doing fine. Same business I've always been in - *health food.*"

I hope you can see that anybody can do this. You can too. You can roam through joke books and find ones that can be personalized to you and strung together into a bit that is truly yours.

Another way to drag out and barely make over and use old jokes and simple gags is by working them into a character. Many won't remember, but rant comedian George Carlin started out as the Hippy-Dippy Weatherman. Sometimes this requires enormous skill. But not always. One of the best examples, presented with great skill, but that would work in many settings if used by a far less skilled performer, was Johnny Carson's Carnac The All-Knowing. Wearing robe and turban, Carson became Carnac. Ed McMahon gave him sealed envelopes in order, asked the questions; Carson tore open the envelopes and read the answers. No memorizing needed. And the gags themselves were often so juvenile they could have been lifted from kids' joke books – and probably were. By the way, don't under-estimate the importance of the straight-man and/or sidekick. Comedy teams like Martin and Lewis, Bob and Ray, the Smothers Brothers, and Johnny and Ed have many advantages over individuals out there all alone, including the ability to use material that would fall flat in monologue, play off each other, direct the audience.

Well, there you have them, six ways to cheat with comedy and get away with it. You can now make yourself appear to be a lot funnier than you really are. Just like your car's side mirror makes objects appear closer than they are. Or three glasses of wine makes women see things as bigger than they are.

Excerpt from the book Here's Johnny! by Ed McMahon

CARNAC THE MAGNIFICENT

I had a special feeling for Carnac the Magnificent, the all-knowing soothsayer from the East with a massive turban who gave questions to the answers I told him. In fact, I kept padding my introduction. I think I peaked on the night that I said,

> And now, bow your heads toward Tibet - and if you don't know where Tibet is, try Pismo Beach - for here he is; that famous sage, soothsayer, and seersucker from the mysterious East; the all-knowing, all-telling, semi-omniscient dress designer to Janet Reno; the borderline sage, would-be-prophet, and Nepalese underachiever...*Carnac the Magnificent!*

And out came Johnny in his oversized robe and preposterous headdress - the towering bejeweled turban that belonged on a seven-foot center. He started wailing toward the desk, missed a step, and grandly fell on his face.

On that particular night, I not only enriched my introduction, but I was able to turn Carnac into heartwarming payback to Johnny for what he had done to me a few weeks before by letting me twist in the wind during an Aunt Blabby sketch.

"Welcome, O Great Sage," I said.

"May a thousand blessings flow across your body," Johnny said.

"That many, O Magnificent One?

"With that body, a thousand might not be enough. May you get your first French kiss from a diseased camel. May a love-starved fruit fly molest your sister's nectarines."

"Abuse from you is like praise from anyone else," I said.

"I don't know what that means, but I know everything else."

"And now the envelope with the answer to the unknown questions," I said, holding it in the air. "I have in my hand, as you can plainly see..."

"Of course I can plainly see, and unfortunately I'm seeing you."

"I said those particular words, O Semidivine One, because sometimes the sand gets in your eyes and..."

"May sand fleas get in your shorts."

"Back to the envelope. A child of six could plainly see that it is hermetically sealed."

"What's that child doing up at midnight?"

"That is not one of your questions, O Semisplendid One. Let me return to the valid questions and say that my daughter, who is four and a half but acts considerably older, can plainly see that the question has been kept in a mayonnaise jar on Funk and Wagnall's porch since noon. No one, absolutely no one --- " And I pounded the desk.

"Carnac may have to call security."

" --- knows its contents!"

"You are right, Large Person," said Johnny. "May those blessings keep flowing over you, with some Gordon's as well."

"O Source of All That Is Wet, O Divine Spigot, we are ready for your first intuition."

"May we have absolute silence, please," he said.

"Many times you have received that," I said, triggering a huge laugh with perhaps the best zinger I had ever thrown on the show.

After letting the laugh play, Johnny said, "Clearly, you have funds put away."

Handing him the envelope, I finally said, "And now, O Great Wind from the East, here is the answer to your first question."

"I was afraid we'd never get to this," Johnny said. "And I was afraid we would."

He pressed the envelope to his forehead and said, "V-8."

"V-8," I said, and Johnny eloquently scowled at me.

And then he opened the envelope and read, "What kind of social disease can you get from an octopus?"

The audience laughed and groaned.

"This audience would lob a grenade at Bambi's mother," Johnny said.

Chapter 8

FUNNY TESTIMONIALS

We all understand the power of testimonials in selling. If this is a foreign concept to you, this is not the most important book for you to be reading at this time.

Sometimes people say funny testimonials – which should be captured, or send funny testimonials – which should be used. I have ones from a guy on vacation, being rowed down an alligator infested river in the jungle, surrounded by magnificent scenery and exotic birds and wildlife, accompanied by a thoroughly annoyed wife, distracted from it all, engrossed in one of my books. Another from a guy who kept finding the Dan Kennedy bobblehead he had on his dresser turned around and facing away from him. His wife confessed to moving it so it wasn't looking at them because she thought I was creepy. Another – with photo of herself in a bikini standing on an elephant – from a female zookeeper who followed my ideas to launch a direct sales company and created such a great income for herself from flexible hours that she could indulge her poorly paying work with animals. And just how many photos from bikini-clad babes standing atop elephants have you been sent?

My two favorites remain these....

> *"I haven't learned as much since Brenda Dillon took me behind a tobacco barn when I was 13 years old."*
>
> *- Bobby Wallace*

> *"....I have NEVER been as excited as I am right now at 2 A.M. This seminar is worth every penny, every back ache, every under-eye bag and dark circle – in fact, if Dan required my next born child in exchange for his information, I'd pay to have a reversal of my tubal ligation..."*
>
> *- Bridget Campbell*

Now, aren't those more interesting to read than the usual "the seminar was the best ever....he was spell-binding....I made millions" stuff? And that's the point: *interest*. If you can't create and keep creating interest, as writer, sales copy writer, salesperson, speaker or entertainer, you're doomed. If you happen to look like Angelina Jolie, interest is easy. Just walk out and stand there. In fact, better you didn't speak. But the rest of us need interesting things said in interesting ways, and that applies not just to what we say but what others say about us that we turn around and use.

If you are very daring, you can also make hay with your negative reviews and complaint letters, which I frequently do. I get so many it'd be criminal to waste such an abundant resource. I have published complaint letters, negative book reviews posted at Amazon, and once delivered an entire 90 minute speech hastily re-crafted as a response to a *complaint letter I received days in advance* of the speech by somebody who had worked himself up to a high level of annoyance anticipating what I was going to say – a first-ever occurrence, by the way, in my 30 year career and possibly in the annals of speaking. Everybody's a critic, but I encountered a psychic critic. Kreskin can find lost objects. Pfui. This guy can hear a yet to be delivered speech days in advance, from thousands of miles away, and get pissed off about it.

Chapter 9

TOASTS AND ROASTS

im McQuillan sent me a note that the toast "Here's mud in your eye" comes from my world of horse racing, from the winner who will be kicking mud into the eyes of those behind him. I did not know that. So here's mud in *your* eye.

The best toast I've ever heard is actor Bob Culp's, for the small, inner circle of Hugh Hefner's friends who've gathered regularly at the Playboy Mansion for poker and movie nights: "Be of good cheer for They are out there and We are in here."

If you are called upon to give a toast, by all means, be brief. It should never take longer to give a toast than it does to *make* toast. Remember, thirsty boozers are waiting for their next drink and you're in the way – and the longer you drone on, the more they need the drink you're delaying. Get out of the way. Here's the right formula: one to two pieces of self-deprecating humor, one or two pieces of humor about the toast-ee, one sincere remark. And out. It's also best to focus the entire toast on one underlying gag. Here's a retirement toast – it entirely focused on the retiree's age:

I appreciate this very undeserved honor, given that my time here at Almagamated Limited has been so short and, frankly, undistinguished – especially compared to Ralph, who began here in the mailroom, feeding and watering the Pony Express horses each day when they arrived. Worked all the way up to the coveted corner cubicle closest to the men's room – which has been very important to him these last few years. Anyway, you've all seen the TV commercials asking: what would you do for a Klondike bar? Now you know. I'm here. Missing the Monday Night game. I know I was not first choice to get our glasses raised to Ralph, but his few friends are all dead. And we better get through this quick; at his age, he has no time to waste. Most people get gold watches at retirement. But Ralph has made so many mistakes here, the company has bronzed an eraser for him. His mind wanders. Wandered. Finally left. So it's time for him to go too. Ralph, we all deeply appreciate your years of unselfish service to this organization and friendship to each and every one of us. To Ralph."

Anything more is not making a toast. It's hogging the spotlight.

Roasts are a much, much, much more complicated thing to pull off or be a part of. The current celebrity roasts done now and then on the Comedy Channel are 80% awful, 10% tedious, 5% embarrassingly and unnecessarily filthy, and 5% brilliant and funny. Bad ratios. You can watch these to see what not to do. By contrast, get the DVD's of the old Dean Martin-hosted celebrity roasts produced by Greg Garrison,

available from Guthy-Renker Corporation (www.guthy-renker.com), and you'll see it done right. Some years ago, we had a premature retirement roast of me. It was put together by Bill Glazer and Steve Tyra. It has not aged well, though, and will likely stay forever sealed in the vault. To the benefit of several of the presenters, notably Doc Nielsen and Joe Polish who discovered it's just not as easy as it looks, this insult humor stuff. I do want to go on record as saying that, at the time, it *was* my intention to speed to retirement. But I changed my mind. What can I say? Me and Brett Favre. Anyway, being asked to be a presenter at a roast actually puts you in a tough spot. Now, you being humorous is not a pleasant surprise for your audience. They *expect* you to be funny.

If you are caught having to speak at a roast, here are my tips:

1: As noted, review Dean Martin Celebrity Roast videos.

2: Know a lot about or thoroughly research and be briefed about the person being roasted; if you are not knowledgeable or willing to do the homework, decline the invitation.

3: If you are to also poke fun at the other roasters, know a lot about or thoroughly research and be briefed about the others on the panel; if you are not knowledgeable or willing to do the homework, decline the invitation.

4: Pull together reliable, generic insult-humor and re-write it for your purposes. (Consider borrowing from: Rickles, Jack E. Leonard, material in Esar's Comic Encyclopedia, Dean Martin roasts).

5: Keep it short. Shorter than your allotted time by a few minutes.

6: Practice, rehearse and preferably memorize your bit. If you're unwilling to do this, decline the invitation.

Here is a brief sample of generic roast material and structure/template....

(1) We are gathered here to honor <insert name>. An obvious mystery. Honoring this man as a <insert status – egs. outstanding citizen/member of x-association, father, coach, whatever> is much like <insert analogy – egs. honoring Britney Spears on Emotional Health Day, giving father of the year award to Alec Baldwin or an Oscar to....>. (2) And why am I here? Have I deep affection or admiration or gratitude to <name>? Do I have

a poignant, personal story to tell about him? I wish. (3) There is no one more boring than <Name>. One time, on a flight, an emergency landing was announced and as the plane dipped downward his entire life started to pass before his eyes – and he dozed off just 2 minutes in. (4) So let's talk about somebody more interesting.....

(5) <Insert one insult-joke for each person on panel>.

(6) Well, I guess I have to say *something* about <Name>. It says so right here on this card (hold up card) that our roast-master <Name> gave me. It says: say something about the Man Of The Hour. Funny, his wife calls him The Man of the Minute. Anyway, this is a tough one. (7) Do I tell you about his brave battle with alcoholism? His dutiful support of his three illegitimate children? All common knowledge. (8) Instead, let me tell you something you may *not* know about <Name>. Something I've personally experienced/witnessed with <Name> that is so revealing of the kind of guy he really is. (9) <Here you need an actual funny story or re-worked joke fitting the person and the roast-occasion i.e. business/career, civic accomplishment, retirement, etc. – here's an example if the person is being honored by a charity:> So we're in this strip club....doing research for <excuse>....and when <Name> heard from Bambi about her mother's desperate need for an operation to save her life and no insurance coverage, he – like the incredibly generous soul he is – literally emptied his wallet and gave her

every dollar he had with him. (Pause). Five dollars at a time. Over the next 4-1/2 hours. (10) We are, of course, all witness to his generosity in this community/organization again and again, so it is, seriously, fitting we honor <Name> tonight, and I'm proud and privileged to do so. (11) And the rest of you should be ashamed of yourselves for making fun of such a fine gentleman. <Name>, on behalf of all the <abandoned pets, starving children, etc.> and occasional stripper you so generously contribute to, thank you.

> *"George and I are both*
> *doing a lot of speaking now.*
> *For money. And I get a higher fee*
> *than he does. There's good reason for that.*
> *I've held my job my whole life and*
> *he's never been able to keep a job*
> *for very long."*
>
> - Barbara Bush, about President George Bush

Look at it for structure: first, the occasion itself made fun of. You could substitute or also make fun of the organization. Second, you lead the audience on a little, suggesting you might be about to praise the roast-ee or say something about your relationship with him, but then you abruptly switch to…third, you insert a joke relevant to the person and dismissive of him. In this example, it's about being boring – appropriate for somebody who is boring. You may want a different negative attribute. Fourth, a bridge to going after the other roasters. Fifth, Jabs at the roast-panelists. Sixth, bridge back to talking about the man of the hour. Seven: fake revelations – pick ones that would be particularly shocking about the person. Note: be sure you know you're on safe ground and not hitting a real nerve. Eighth, bridge to your main story/joke. Nine: shift to serious, sincere praise. Ten: end with a final joke. And get off the stage.

The example I constructed here is far from brilliant, but it would be serviceable in many situations. However, I'm not selling the actual material here, just illustrating a structure you can use to build any presentation as a roaster you need. And if you need to expand its length, you'd do that in (5) – with two pokes instead of one at each panelist, or taking more time with one with whom you have more of a relationship than the others; and/or (9) – with two stories instead of one, making sure the second one connects to the (10) you need.

If you must organize a roast, my best piece of advice is to get suddenly called out of the country on a lengthy, top secret CIA mission, send your apologies telegram from Casablanca, and stay over there sipping Mai-tai's and playing gin rummy until the whole thing is over. But if you must….

Put together the right people for your panel. You need roasters who can be funny but will take the task seriously and prepare and be prepared. Do not turn them loose – work with them individually and as a group to get the best material put together you possibly can. If a budget exists, consider hiring a comedy writer. Even someone who's a beginner at stand-up, perhaps working at your local comedy club, can be very helpful. Give every roaster this Chapter and Chapter 7 of this book. Make sure the M-C is the best possible person, and, again, consider hiring a pro. Put your strongest panelists first and last; weakest in the middle. Run a rehearsal. Have a brief open-bar cocktail hour *for the audience* beforehand. Finally, have the host or M-C give the audience its instructions – example:

> Welcome to tonight's Roast of our good friend and deserved honoree, uh (look at card)...John, uh, Fundermink. We have # panelists tonight who have worked very hard to prepare their remarks about John and to entertain you. These are not professional comedians. I've been to rehearsal. I can assure you, they are <u>not</u> professional comedians. But this is a comedy roast – or not – depending more on you than them. Johnny Carson said that comedy is delivered by comedians but lives or dies in the hands of the audience. So it's all up to you. Whether we have a great time tonight or not is up to you – and the person sitting on either side of you, so if they aren't laughing, jab 'em in the ribs, and while they're distracted, you might as well steal their wallets. We're all here to have a good time at John's expense. Let's do it! Now, direct from the Accounting Department in the basement – and where else would you look for funny? – the life of the party, Charlie Waters....

This is, incidentally, a combination of comedian Shelley Berman's opening instruction to his audiences and an 'agreements process' from human potential training seminars. There are lots of variations. There is, for example, the telling the audience that tonight's humor is very high-brow and only audiences of great intelligence and will get it.

You can help your panelists. Refer to Chapter 7 on Cheating, and by all means, cheat. In between panelists, you can show funny photos or video of the roast-ee, acquired from family, from the company picnic, etc., captioned, dubbed with music or news-announcer voice-over. A hired funny character can be brought in - a drunken bimbo who staggers in looking for the roast-ee, finding him, parking on his lap, demanding to know why he's kept her waiting up in the room. A young mother carrying a baby demanding her past due child support. A process server. A klutz waiter. At the semi-retirement roast that was very prematurely done for me, they had a "dead on" Ruth Buzzi bag-lady from Laugh-In impersonator burst in, take the podium, deliver a funny monologue and whack me silly with her purse. As long as these 'extras' are brief and interspersed, don't worry about up-staging your panelists. The trade-off of getting the audience "in fun" and laughing is worth it, because it builds on itself.

The toughest thing is being roasted. You can only partially prepare, but you need to be able to respond to the unknown as well. There are two basic things to do to prepare and go in prepared. First, write several insult-jokes for each of the roasters that you may be able to use regardless of what they say. Ideally, you need only a note or two and the punch line for each, not the whole joke written out, so you can condense these onto one 4x6" card for each roaster. Second, put together some generic insult-jokes that can be used "depending on", and moved around as needed. These need to be one per card, and these cards should be a different color card stock than the first group, so it's easy to keep them separated. Of course, you want blank cards and felt-tips with you, to jot notes as each roaster does his presentation.

The two most difficult situations you'll face are: a roaster who has been horribly un-funny and flopped; one who has been very, very uncomfortably inappropriate, profane or offensive.

To the first: it's nearly impossible to ignore it. So you have to open with piling on to the poor guy's failure. Example: *Every since they put Bob on anti-depressants, he's been a helluva lot funnier, don't you think?* Or: *Bob. Bob. Didn't you get the memo? This was supposed to be a COMEDY roast.* Or: *Your wife Helen said you couldn't possibly be more dull and boring than you were on your honeymoon. She was wrong. Helen – you owe me twenty bucks.* Then do whatever material you planned for poor Bob. At the end, you may choose to rehab him a little, say a couple nice things and tell him how much you appreciate him.

To the second: again, it's nearly impossible to ignore it. If you like prop humor, carry a small bar of soap in your pocket, walk over to Bob The Pottymouth, make a big show of handing him the soap and tell him he has a little job to do later – *with his mouth.* Or: *Gee, it looks like Bob took that two drink minimum thing seriously and decided to be a big over-achiever.* Or: *On Bob's behalf, I'd like to apologize to the ladies in the room.* Put hand over eyes, scan the room… *oops, there aren't any. We'll just move on.* Then do whatever material you planned for poor Bob. At the end, you may choose to rehab him a little, say a couple nice things and tell him how much you appreciate him.

In a few roasts, the roast-ee gets up and fires back after each roaster, but it is more common for the roast-ee – you – to get one shot, last. You are not bound by the order the roasters presented in. Start with some general comment, like this one from comedy writer Bob Orben: *This has definitely been 'an evening to remember'. I say an evening to remember because I want to get it right when I talk to my lawyer in the morning.* Then take each person in whatever order seems best/funniest to you. If somebody mis-behaved or flopped, you probably want to get them done first. End with whomever you think you have the best/funniest material for.

The most important thing to remember is that you are being watched the entire time. You can never let yourself display anger or annoyance or boredom (although if someone is droning on, you can make a big show of checking your watch, checking it against the watch of the person next to you). You *have to* laugh and be in fun and be a very good sport, no matter what. Get your revenge later.

Chapter 10

INTRODUCING A SPEAKER, BEING INTRODUCED AS A SPEAKER

I'm sorry to disappoint you: in most situations, this is **not** the time and place to demonstrate your comedic genius.

When you are introducing a speaker, it is about them, not you.

The person delivering an introduction needs to understand what is needed to best enhance the speaker's effectiveness. That may be establishing his expert authority and status, his direct relevance to the audience, or his purpose for being there. It may be erasing some skepticism or resistance about the material the speaker will be presenting. It may be setting up the sale of resources. It may require a recital of resume in as interesting a way as possible, a personal testimonial, a testimonial from someone in the group or the industry the audience is in. Ideally, the speaker you are tasked with introducing has clear objectives and can

115

discuss them with you to strategize for success, and, of course, provide information for you to work from.

Rarely can you best serve the speaker's objectives by getting up in front of him and attempting to be funny. Or *being* funny. But if you insist on doing so, at least avoid like the plague any humor that is at all derogatory or diminishing of the speaker – whether joking about the tie he's wearing or something more significant. Your job is to raise his stature, not sabotage it or put it at risk. Also take care not to use a joke or story he relies on. If you're not sure, check with the speaker about the story you intend using in advance.

If you want to be *a little funny*, consider making fun of what your speaker *isn't.* Example:

> I know you've been in way too many sales meetings with egghead theorists who are about as useful to real salespeople as the sex expert who can diagram 52 different positions but has never even had a date. Our speaker today has 25 years' of real, successful experience and is street-smart. By the way, you know MBA stands for More Bad Advice. There's a new designation: MBA – WAS. Stands for an MBA Working At Starbucks. Well, our speaker, John Jones, probably wouldn't even be allowed onto a college campus, but you're gong to be very happy he came here because…

The expert/consultant line is very old, and fairly reliable. The MBA-WAS is my very own invention, and also pretty reliable with groups who don't hold those with MBA's in high regard. MBA's never laugh at it. Or at much of anything else. The 'formula' is: have a little fun with a 'target' the group doesn't like or respect, that is the antithesis of the speaker you're introducing.

Key word I've used here repeatedly is: **little.** Do NOT turn your introduction into your audition for the comedy club. Get it done. Get the speaker up there.

If you are a speaker who sells, your introduction and the person giving it are both critically important, so you ought not leave either to random chance, nor take any of the above for granted. We pro speakers all have many 'war stories' of horrific introductions that put us at great disadvantage and stole a lot of money from us. We learn to exert as much control as we possibly can. Some speakers create introductory DVD's to be played as their main intro, reducing the human introducer to the briefest of opportunities to do harm, and delivering a perfectly produced, exciting intro with video of their exploits, shots of them with famous celebrities, sometimes even quick testimonials. A few comedians do this too – I've witnessed it in Vegas showrooms.

If you intend making the audience laugh, the introduction is a golden opportunity to convey that expectation. Your introducer can say something like…

Now, I have to warn everybody, Billy Speaker is very funny. I guess you might not think about this subject (insert topic) as being ripe with humor, but when I've seen Billy speak (watched Billy on DVD) I laughed a lot. You will too. But don't let the humor mask the importance of what he has to say about…

If you are an introducer, and your speaker uses humor, you should include some conveyance of expectation like this in your introduction.

If you are a speaker with a DVD shown as part of your introduction, make sure it includes you in front of a big audience that is roaring with laughter.

The best introductions for a speaker who sells mix the carefully crafted material built for the standard intro with a personal story/testimonial from the introducer. If the event has an M-C who can't do that for you, try to switch the situation, so the M-C intro's somebody from the group who, in turn, introduces you, and can give personal endorsement.

As an aside, here's the answer to how to get laughs, from long-time live show and TV producers Harry King and Lee Laufer: *you say funny things in a funny fashion to an audience that has been primed for laughter.* The last 1/3rd of that formula is very important. How the audience is "primed" matters a great deal. If they are primed to pay attention as if their lives or making of their hoped-for millions depended on it....primed to forgive a little coarseness and profanity.....primed to find the speaker hilarious, and to relax, let loose and have a helluva good time.... the speaker benefits. To have fun, an audience must be "in fun". A skilled humorist or comic can get them there from scratch, 'cold', himself, but it's not easy and it takes time away from the actual presentation. It's much better if they're already there. What precedes the speaker who intends using humor, and what is said introducing him, can be of great help or do great harm.

ATTENTION MEETING ORGANIZERS AND HOSTS: if you are sharing in a speaker's sales revenues, you are a nitwit if you fail to invest time, thought, energy and cooperation in getting this right. The effectiveness of the introduction(s) will impact the selling effectiveness of the speaker(s). If you *read* the intro – especially if you supposedly know or work with the speaker and are giving personal endorsement – you discredit yourself and the speaker. Memorize your intro. Then just have reminder notes. But don't read word for word from a page. It looks like shit. Either invest time personally in doing your intros well, or assign them to people who will. Incidentally, letting key people, members, etc. in your group "have the honor of" introducing speakers is a terrific way to involve people, give recognition, and delegate this work. If you do, make them read this Chapter of this book.

Frankly, most give all this short shrift and screw themselves and their speakers.

The 4 Worst Mood-Killing Introductions of My Career

(1): A multi-level/network marketing group:

"Before we get started tonight, folks, I'm afraid I have some bad news. Late this afternoon, our company finally folded under pressure from the attorney generals in 4 states and we will be filing for bankruptcy and ceasing operations tomorrow. Bonus checks just issued will be void. I really don't have any more information for you at this time. But since we're all here anyway, and Mr. Kennedy has traveled all the way from Phoenix to be here, we might as well go ahead with tonight's program…"

(2): A corporate gig:

"Before I introduce our great speaker this morning, I have some news. After his long and painful battle with anal cancer, our beloved CEO died last night, and we are going to have a moment of silent prayer in his honor. Will you dim the lights, please…."

(3): An evening association gig in downtown Wichita, Kansas:

"Before we get started with Mr. Kennedy, I have to tell you – and him – that we've just gotten word of a massive winter storm set to descend on this area within the hour. Y'all know how brutal these things can be. Probably going to get 3 feet dumped on us. It's a good thing we're in a hotel, huh? We might be stuck here. Ha-ha. Anyway, as soon as Mr. Kennedy finishes, you'll want to skip the coffee and hurry on outta here…"

(4): A corporate gig, first thing in the morning:

"Well, here we are. At 8:00 A.M. I really don't know why we needed to get up early to listen to another one of these damned *motivational* speakers, but I drew the short straw, so let me tell you about him…"

Chapter 11

BEING GOOD-HUMORED VS. BEING HUMOROUS

or most business purposes, as a speaker, or in writing, being good-humored is enough. You don't actually need to be funny. You just need for the audience to like you and have some fun with you.

"If I get BIG laughs, I'm a comedian.
If I get small laughs, I'm a humorist.
If I get no laughs - I'm a singer."

- George Burns

Bob Farrell is that kind of a speaker. He created Farrell's Ice Cream Parlors in Akron, Ohio, sold out to Marriott for a pot of dough, and became sort of a customer service evangelist. His main speech, available as a book, is titled *"Give 'Em The Pickle"*, which ties to a story about a customer at Farrell's. His speech is full of good-humored stories unlikely to have people rolling in the aisles, but good enough to get nods, smiles and chuckles, and loaded with homespun, whimsical sayings.

A saying like *"The people who tell you not to worry about the little things have never tried sleeping in a room with a mosquito."* A story like: *"One Saturday night I had two ambitious busboys working who were high school track stars. They were having fun trying to clean the tables before I pointed it out to them. One time they yelled out, 'Table 21 cleaned, Mr. Farrrell'. No sooner had I seated four people at that table than the four who had been sitting there came out of the restroom looking for their table – and food. They hadn't finished their meal yet."*

No, that stuff isn't gonna put an audience into convulsions. But being homespun and using clever and whimsical phrases to make your points will make you more listenable and entertaining, and will get the audience on your side. The amusing, quick story works much the same way. And you don't have to be a pro comic to do this.

Mike Vance is even a better example and every speaker should get and listen to every Vance recording – but there is an audio program of just his best stories. He is a masterful storyteller. All kinds. Poignant. Tear-jerker. Good-humored. Occasionally humorous. But only rarely, very rarely, outright funny.

I think the worst speakers for audiences are the all business, all meat 'n potatoes, content overwhelm guys. I started out as one of them. You got more meat per minute than from any speaker – in fact, I advertised that and bragged about it. Problem is, there aren't a lot of steak lovers who just want to chow down on a 5-pound steak with no accompaniments. Most want a salad, some potatoes, maybe a couple onion rings, bread. I gradually arrived at a target of conveying three main pieces of information or instruction per hour and no more, all wrapped up in and accompanied by entertainment – not a comedy act in most cases, but some humor, and some good-humored storytelling. People are much more "into" stories than they are information, and a heck of a lot happier with entertainment than with education.

The same thing is true with writing. My first two business books, *The Ultimate Sales Letter* and *The Ultimate Marketing Plan*, were, in first editions, very straightforward, 1-2-3 how-to books. Fortunately for me, they are so damned useful (!) they survived and have had remarkably long lives, uninterrupted space on bookstore shelves since 1991 and 1993 respectively, out-living tens of thousands of how-to books. In subsequent, revised editions, I injected a little personality and made them a little more friendly. But my *NO B.S.* books are very different. They are good-humored throughout, and humorous in parts, built in much the same ratio as my speeches. And each time I've revised them, I've moved further away from 'what to do and how to do it' to saying funny things in a funny way, that at least get nods, smiles, chuckles and, sometimes, gasps. And these books are much, much more successful – in total, now topping 200,000 copies sold.

Chapter 12

WORD CANDY

 phrase like "*nuttier than grandma's fruitcake*" is more interesting than simply saying: he's nuts. It's not laugh out loud funny. It's whimsical. And then you can play around with it, to try making it better. *Nuttier than grandma's unwanted fruitcake. Nuttier than grandma's dried apricot-and-weird-green-things, pecan, cinnamon and ground-granite fruit cake.* And so on.

When writing advertising or sales copy, particularly long copy, picking places to replace ordinary verbiage with these kinds of enhanced phrases can help keep the reader interested and even help put him in a good mood, more receptive to buying. You can't over-do it or it loses its effectiveness. But here and there, throughout copy, throwing in some word candy helps the message go down.

WHY PEOPLE FAIL TO BE FUNNY

"THE PROBLEM WITH HUMOR WRITING IS – you have to know how to write. That takes years of practicing the craft, of honing your skills, rewriting. Rework the writing until it's funny. ....writing humor takes discipline and hard work. I have this theory. Here it is, My Theory About Writing: it's hard. The humor doesn't just flow. A funny idea has to be tooled and shaped so it's funny to others when it's read (or heard)".....To make sure the joke works..."I spend a lot of time reading every sentence over and over, focusing on details. I mean small details, like word choice. Very often, that's what's going to determine whether an idea is funny. It can be as detailed as using the word 'got' instead of 'received,' for example."

- Drew Carey, from the book HOW TO WRITE FUNNY

In speaking, the same kind of word candy can also hold the interest of and amuse an audience. Details matter. There's a big difference between saying you entered a room or went into a restaurant or drove across a bridge and describing that act and that place in a way that is funny and that puts the listener or reader right there in the experience with you. The difference is being dull and bland or interesting and humorous. Consider the difference between *telling of* driving across a toll-bridge and *describing* the crossing of the toll bridge – and the bridge itself – as comedian Ron White does in this routine:

...the only way to get there is across this rickety little wooden toll bridge. And the toll to cross this bridge is six bucks. To cross a little rickety fucking bridge. I expected there to be a troll and some billy goats or something. And I make a lot of money. Not doing comedy. I sell shrimp out of a van. But six bucks seems like a lot of money, And then when you get up to the little cage where you pay the toll, I swear to God it's true, there's a little sign that says, "No coins or cash." What do they want you to pay them with - a hand job?

He goes on to talk about getting pulled over for speeding on the bridge - doing 7 MPH in a 5 MPH zone. Begging the cop to slap on the handcuffs and take him away. He'll make a million dollars telling the story.

By the way, most comedians would consider a night in the local clink a small price to pay for a good piece of material. And, for the record, a true friend does not come over and bail you out. He rushes over, pees on the deputy's shoes so he gets thrown in the cell with you, and you have somebody to watch your back and swap jokes with all night.

A bit like Ron's does not write itself. The incident undoubtedly occurred, Ron recognized its potential, then invested time and effort in experimenting with telling it one way versus another, using this phrase or that. The reference to trolls is inspired, in Ron's case, possibly by alcohol. Ultimately, this is a developed piece of material, that gets locked into memory and told verbatim again and again.

Chapter 13

HUMOR WRITING

riting humorous articles, essays or books is a much more difficult job than writing humor and then delivering it live – the writing must be read, and you can't inject voice inflection and tone, pauses and timing, or gestures.

There was a time when there were a lot of humorous essayist and columnists, and a lot of humor published. Robert Benchley and Dorothy Parker leap to mind. And if you're ever in New York, you should visit or stay at The Algonquin, home of the original Dorothy Parker Roundtable, where the literary lions, satirists, humorists and wits of the time met for weekly sparring matches over tea and booze and crumpets. I'm afraid these days, watching a battle of wits amongst most writers would prove pretty dull. There is a game show called *'Show Us Your Wits'* on the Playboy Channel, though, that's amusing. Anyway, humor writing is a disappearing genre. There is a humor section at your local Barnes & Noble and you ought to visit it and raid it, but most of the books by comedians are merely their live acts transcribed and cut up into chapters.

Well worth having and studying. But not from-scratch humor writing of essays just to be read. In that shrinking space, one of the last, best men standing is Dave Barry. You can find a number of books with his collected newspaper columns, however the book you must get and read that is wonderful demonstration of satirical comedy authorship – and will be fun for you to read, is *Dave Barry's Money Secrets*. It purports to be an instructional/how-to book all about money, something like Suze Orman or Dave Ramsey might churn out. It is written in that tone. But it is viciously funny.

What is instructional is that much of it deals with topics most comedians use at one time or another, yet Dave found different ways to plumb it. Like this, about the I.R.S. tax code we all love so dear…

Congress has no idea what's in the U.S. Tax Code……but let's not be too harsh on Congress. Nobody understands the U.S. Tax Code, It's far too difficult even for really smart people. Back in 1955, Albert Einstein, acting on a dare from some fellow geniuses at a genius party, attempted to read the Tax Code, and within minutes he keeled over dead. 'His brain looked like tapioca,' the coroner said. And that was fifty years ago when the Tax Code was only a few million words. It's much bigger now – so big that nobody dares go near it. It's kept in a locked, windowless vault in the basement of the Internal Revenue Service building. Every day at 3 p.m. a taxpayer is selected at random, audited, then thrown into this vault. There's a scream, followed by silence, followed by a massive burp. The next day the Tax Code is bigger.

This is a funny bit that could be delivered live, but that reads well. If you dissect it, you'll find it carefully built. The first sentences state the premise, just as Speaking Rule #1 in 101 Class dictates: tell 'em what you're going to tell them. It's a good rule for writing, too. People need to know where you're taking them, kind of like they need to see the picture on the box of the product they're expected to assemble inside. The use of Einstein is brilliant. **The detail there is important.** *A genius party?* Who knew there were such things? That alone is a funny idea – did your mind instantly make you a little picture when you first read it? Einstein and the other geniuses dancing to records or playing Twister®? Reading the Tax Code turning his brain to tapioca (not the clichéd "mush"; tapioca) and killing him gives you another little picture or two. And the end has you seeing the Tax Code as a giant monster eating taxpayers and burping in satisfaction after each meal.

Is this kind of writing important for you? I think so. I strive for it in my newsletters, books, faxes and blogs. These days, every business and its owner has at its disposal more media, and that media demands more writing, and for it to hold anybody's interest, it needs to be witty writing. Not to suggest I'm in Dave Barry's league, still, if you take this passage above written by Barry and keep it handy while you go to your collection of *No B.S. Marketing Letters* and review a few month's of opening monologues, Renegade Millionaire Back Pages; the other newsletters; and, if a Diamond Member, the weekly faxes, I believe you'll find quite a bit of writing that compares favorably. It's neither accident nor natural talent oozing out onto the pages. It is deliberate.

This, incidentally, is why delegating **your** writing for **your** communications with **your** customers to some starving student in Bangladesh found on e-lance, who'll do a dozen articles for six rupees, is such a bad idea. Yes, it can help get you to that 4-hour workweek. But at what price? And, what business are you in, anyway? For the record, 'cuz people ask: everything in every one of the newsletters that is attributed to me is written by me and not recycled from past material, either. I write the weekly faxes. I write my own blog posts. I write my own books. There's often some jealous dimwit somewhere on the internet spreading the rumor that I use ghost-writers or that there are staff writers or that I've been dead for 6 months and somebody else is regurgitating my old stuff or some such idiocy. Pfui.

One final word about this – don't just pick up a couple books by somebody like Dave Barry and copycat his style or worse, that, plus swiping his material. Or mine. Find your own voice. Most people have a sense of humor – except militant feminists, hard-core leftist liberals like Barbra Streisand, attorneys who make less than $35,000.00 a year and Dick Cheney. You just need to *use* yours.

Some Examples of some hopefully funny stuff or stuff said in a funny way, in my books:

In *No B.S. Ruthless Management of People & Profits:* Chapter 1, pages 1-8 (making fun of academic management theorists and a college brochure. Includes The Diversity Fight Song). Page 10 (employer/employee conflicting agendas). Page 136 (re. GE-Spot vs. G-Spot). Pages 241-242 (self-deprecating story re. Do-Doing-Done). If you go back and read through all the No B.S. books for purpose of spotting all the uses of humor, the different types of jokes used, etc. you'll see everything presented here, in this book, done - and if I say so myself - done well. It'd be a good idea to buy new copies of all these books, so you can mark them up with hi-liters just for this purpose. Buy books. I have racehorses to feed. Info's at www.NoBSBooks.com. In *My Unfinished Business:* Chapters 11 & 12 - pages 62-68 (about cars). Chapter 34 - Pages 174-178 (about travel). Pages 182-185 (about being a celebrated author). Pages 282-291 (about marriage). Note: page numbers from Glazer-Kennedy Advantage edition of the book. In *Uncensored Sales Strategies:* pages 113-124 (section titled: *If You Use Brute Force, Don't Expect A Lot Of Valentine's Day Cards*). I have guest chapters in this book; it is written by Sydney Barrows, and at my suggestion, the entire book is full of word play and innuendo, having fun with her past illicit business life as the famous Mayflower Madam - while drawing useful selling lessons from it. She did a masterful job writing this book "in fun" and its publisher, Entrepreneur Press, played along nicely with the cover design and interior graphics.

Vincent Palko
www.AdToons.com

"Rule #10:

Try to leave out the part that readers tend to skip."

- Elmore Leonard,

from Elmore Leonard ms 10 Rules of Writing

Chapter 14

EVERGREEN COMEDY

uman folly is never fixed, so much of comedy stays evergreen, and very old material can easily be dusted off and easily brought up-to-date, or even used as is.

This is from 1975. Originally written to make fun of *foreign* cars:

Some of these cars are so small – how small are they? – they're so small they have to be home before dark. This afternoon at the mall parking lot I saw two of these little cars parked under a station wagon. I didn't know if they were hiding or nursing. One good thing: if you run out of gas, you don't have to walk to the gas station, get a gas can and walk back; you just carry the car there under your arm.

Easily buffed up to make fun of the new "smart cars". And this 1975 joke still works too:

Last month a Japanese spy stole secret plans from General Motors. This month, 87,000 Toyotas were recalled.

For those of you who went to public school, those jokes are 34 years old, as of this writing, courtesy, Harry King. Only Hostess Twinkies® have that kind of shelf life.

> *"A man is being interviewed on his 100th birthday on* The Today Show. *Willard Scott asks him how he lived to be 100. The guy says, 'First you get to be 99. Then you have to be careful as hell for a year.'* "
>
> *- Herb True*

Money is another subject safe from age.

Again, from Harry's joke book circa 1975: *money is not important to me at all. I only need money if I don't die.* Health the same – this from Phil Harris: *if I'd known I was going to live this long, I'd have taken better care of myself.*

There are mountains of easily recycleable material about "the basic subjects": Money, Health, Age, Marriage, Sex, and about the "everydays": Cars, Travel, Vacations. When you stick to the basic categories, you have a ton of material to choose from, swipe, easily tweak and use, and you connect with your audience in a fundamental way.

Everybody's had a family vacation go bad. Not everybody can identify with the agony of being waited on by a poorly skilled sommelier. Everybody has a know-it-all, douche-bag brother-in-law. Not everybody has a butler. Everybody has a Ralph Kramden in the family, constantly coming up with some new, outlandish get-rich-quick scheme. Oh, but wait a minute, that's you in your family, isn't it? Anyway, the point is, stay in a play area everybody's familiar with and that essentially never changes, year to year, generation to generation. (By the way, if it never dawned on you that The Flintstones was a direct swipe of The Honeymooners, go watch a couple original Honeymooners episodes, then a few Flintstones episodes. It's instructive.)

If you feel like you want to twist the evergreen stuff a little, try the fish out of water or stranger in a strange land gambit. Think: Beverly Hillbillies. Or even more on spot: Green Acres. You, transplanted to some setting the audience is familiar with, but you aren't, allows you to make fun of them in a way they enjoy, and to make fun of yourself too. This can be as simple as the new, first-time father describing his new discoveries in parenthood, to an audience of older, married folks who all have kids. The long-time bachelor describing his discoveries about marriage – a schtick Seinfeld does now beautifully. Buddy Hackett had a bit where he tried explaining marriage to Martians who'd just landed on earth. I have a bit about the first person who tried telling me about chiropractic, which kills with audiences of chiropractors. Slays 'em. That's obviously very specific material for a very specific audience, but the principle's the same: something the audience is familiar with and takes for granted, shown to them as hilarious and strange or even scary through the eyes of the "Martian".

Who uses Evergreen Comedy? Everybody. Ron White's act includes bits about buying sunglasses and buying tires from Sears, having a radio stolen from his car and dealing with the insurance company, his wife's terrible cooking, his dog...just stated this way, it all sounds very ordinary, doesn't it? It is. And that's the beauty of it. We all own this kind of material and can rely on it. It's a solid and safe foundation.

> *"Never play peek-a-boo with a child*
> *on a long airplane trip.*
> *There's no end to the game.*
> *Finally I grabbed him by the bib and said,*
> *'Look. It's always going to be me.'"*
>
> *- Rita Rudner*

Chapter 15

FORTUNATELY FOR US, GOD CREATED LAWYERS, POLITICIANS AND BUREAUCRATS

o you dare question God? Did we really need mosquitoes? If so, did they need to want our blood? And carry disease? Well, at least it's obvious why he permitted there to be lawyers, politicians and bureaucrats – to make the rest of us feel so much better about ourselves. But did they need to want our blood? And carry disease?

You canmt lose with making fun of authority figures

Government bureaucrats, for example. Is there a comedian who hasn't done a bit about the Department of Motor Vehicles folks? Or the Post Office? More imaginatively, there's the story of the agents on the combined DEA, ATF and FBI Task Force combing the rural areas of the dust bowl states for pot farms, meth labs and other illicit activity – just like the revenuers of old. So, three of these agents; the FBI guy in a grey suit, the DEA guy in a brown suit, and the ATF guy in a blue suit arrive in a 4-door Chevy in a cloud of dust at this farm out in the middle of nowhere, accost the farmer, and tell him that they are there to inspect the entire farm….every square inch…for suspected drug production.

Farmer shrugs and says, "Fine, fellers, but you probably ought skip that pasture over there next to the red barn."

"Now listen here mister," the DEA agent blusters, "we are here backed by the full force and authority of the United States government and we are authorized to go everywhere and anywhere we want on your farm."

The FBI agent produces his badge and proudly displays it. "See this badge, old-timer? It means you can't tell us where we can and can't go."

The ATF guy says, "Stand aside."

And they stomp off toward the pasture by the red barn.

In just a few minutes, the farmer hears their loud screams and yelling for help. He wanders over and finds them running for their lives around the pasture with his prize rodeo bull, 'Killer', gaining on them with every step. And the farmer hollers –

"Show him your badge!"

Works most places, but *kills* in small towns and rural areas. I got it from a guy who made a living as an after-dinner speaker for electrical co-ops, Farm Bureau groups and Knife & Fork Clubs. If all that is unfamiliar to you, consider yourself lucky.

Lawyers are the easiest targets. Lawyer jokes abound. There are big, thick books just of lawyer jokes – help yourself. But be forewarned: entrepreneurs and executives can't hear enough of 'em, but lawyers do take offense at them, unless told by other lawyers. Kinda like Chris Rock being able to use the N word, and call his black audience a bunch of, well you know, but I can't. Lawyers are *very* sensitive, with good reason: guilt and shame. So be careful. They can sue. I have made a lot of fun of lawyers and said a lot of mean and cruel things about them during my 30 years of speaking and writing, and offended and hurt many – ***and this is as good a time and place as any to say how deeply I regret it.*** I so wish I could have found or thought up more. I did the best I could, as much as I could, as often as I could, but I still feel I've come up short. And I regret it.

Politicians are the gift that keeps on giving albeit at considerable cost to us all. Sarah Palin's reach for foreign relations credibility because she can see Russia from her porch. Obama's much bigger catalog of idiotic pronouncements, notably including his assertion that, if we all just kept our tires properly inflated, that would do as much as drilling for more oil. Biden's characterization of Obama during the campaign as "neat and clean". Sanford's stroll down the Appalachian Trail all the way to Argentina where his mistress lived. Pretty-boy Edwards' refusal to even acknowledge the existence of his mistress' new-born baby despite the photo of him holding it in his arms, and Mrs. Edwards' insistence that there must be a lot of photos from the campaign trail of John holding and kissing babies. Hard to find more than one of him seated in a chair in a hotel room with a tyke in his arms, though. Cheney shooting his lawyer-friend in the face while quail hunting.

There are a few things to keep in mind about reaching into the rich, deep, daily replenishing cesspool of political material...

First, this is where the pros go. They plumb these depths daily. So you are butting heads here with the late night show monologists, with Jon Stewart and Stephen Colbert, with the top comedy writers in the country. Don't swipe; people will catch it, and think a lot less of you. If you use these folks and their foolishness, you'd better be sure it's good stuff and you're good at delivering it.

Second, you have to decide whether or not to be partisan. Carson famously hid his politics and balanced the blows delivered nightly to both sides of the aisle, so you could not be certain if he was liberal or conservative or agnostic, and it wasn't easy to get angry at him over poking at your guys when he was poking at theirs too. The next generation, Leno and Letterman, are clearly partisan. Letterman more blatant than Leno. Personally, there are places and times where I balance so I can tap into peoples' frustration with all politicians without significant risk of offending significant numbers in an audience. At other times, I choose to make my own beliefs and agenda abundantly clear – some of those times because I know the overwhelming majority there share my views; some of those times because I don't give a damn who I offend. I'm always conscious of it, though. In advertising, it's more dangerous, but can be effective. One of the very first full-page ads I ever wrote, in early 70's, referred to the Watergate cover-up. The full-page ad I wrote for Jeff Paul's book had a PS about Hillary coming for all your money, and we tested, and the PS did bump response – although we took it out when we ran the ad in *Mother Earth News*, the official journal of tree-hugging Birkenstock® wearers who live off the grid, churning butter out back.

Third, politics is very fluid. I do my weekly column, as of this writing, over the weekend, to move to its publisher on Monday, to appear on Wednesday. A lot can happen between Sunday and Wednesday, so I have to be careful not to be too specific about anything, and to choose stories that "have legs". Shelf life for political *jokes* can be very limited. On the other hand, the shelf life of political *humor* is very long. Mark Twain made a living with it, and much of his material could be used today, only with names and places changed to spotlight the currently guilty. Here's a very generic joke from comedy writer Bob Orben's pen, circa 1976:

I just saw a classified ad. 'For Sale: U.S. Treasury. Take over payments'.

Today, it could be:

I was on eBay the other day, looking for a good price on Erik Estrada memorabilia for my collection, when I saw this: For Sale: U.S. Treasury. No Money down. Take over payments.

Or you could substitute Craigslist for eBay, and if you chose, work in reference to all the prostitutes who advertise there, so it's appropriate the politicians are advertising their wares there too. In fact, here's another interesting ad: *Hot Argentinean Bombshell, former mistress of American politician, summarily displaced, now available. Seeks good-looking guy with a sense of humor, a lot of frequent flier miles, and no bitchy wife.* Funnier if you pop up a photo of a very hot Argentinean babe in a bikini, holding up a sign that says 'America Or Bust.' Just remember, as I cautioned, the opener about the ad selling the U.S. Treasury is evergreen; the reference to Gov. Sanford's excellent Argentina adventure is not. It's probably dated here.

You could turn it into a bit made up of funny eBay or Craigslist ads, and go in a direction other than politics. You could go from it to a list of stupid stuff the government has been spending its money on – like loaning $538-million to Al Gore's car company, to develop a luxury hybrid that will sell for $90,000.00, with all the R&D work being done thus jobs created in Finland. You can't make that shit up. Only from the fertile mind of the man who invented the Internet and melting ice caps could come such an ingenious business plan. Bernie Madoff turned to his cellmate and said, "Sonofabitch, why didn't I think of that?"

If you're comedy challenged, you could use the Leno/Headlines cheat, and get the gag ads made up graphically, to show up on the screen. Or get photos – for the above opener, of the U.S. Treasury Building, with a photo-shopped For Sale sign in front of it.

Any or all of this made from one old but undamaged by age one-liner.

Chapter 16

ANGRY RANT COMEDY

I imagine there was somebody at The Last Supper doing 5 minutes on the annoying things that happened at temple.

Pretty much, everybody's pissed off at the same people and same things. But even if you rage against something relatively unique, you'll find that people *like* an outraged, angry man. We all hate the bastards who package things inside impossible to open and penetrate packaging – especially if what's inside is the thing needed to get inside, like, say, a knife or pair of scissors. Not everybody hates men who talk on cell phones while standing at urinals in public restrooms and peeing, but if I get worked up about it, an audience will find it and my outrage funny.

There have been many great rant comedians. Sam Kinison's rants about his ex-wives and about people whining and complaining about being poor and homeless and put upon are absolute masterpieces, and screamingly funny, although very, very profane. Lewis Black is a superb rant comedian. Some people say that I remind of him when I'm going off about something, and I take it as a great compliment. Dennis Miller, of course, made a living for a while as a pure rant guy – beginning each bit with "I don't want to go off on a rant here, but…" Carlin morphed into a rant comedian. His last HBO specials are strung together rants – like his list of ten kinds of people who deserve to have their heads bashed in with heavy objects, setting up mini-rants about people who pull out baby pictures at cocktail parties and have "My Son Is A A-Student" bumper stickers, celebrities who adopt third-world babies, and militant political correctness enforcers.

Some take this too far and start taking themselves way too seriously, and stop being funny. Lenny Bruce. Bill Maher. You can clearly see Maher's future as a bitter has-been yelling at kids to get the f*** off his lawn. If you want to study models in this category, stick with the ones who have a sense of humor. Lewis Black may be the best of the current crop.

Most comedians at least rant a little. Seinfeld's routine about the car rental counter is for road warriors who deal with such abuse all the time. It's 'rant lite.' *You can take a reservation, but apparently you can't keep a reservation.* The ills of travel have long offered reliable rant material – as long as the audience travels a lot. Shelley Berman's routine about hotels was so good it got turned into a book all by itself, titled *'A Hotel Is A Place'.* I leapt off from it for my little list about hotels in *Unfinished Business.*

If you want to rant, any target will do, as long as it's not so obscure nobody connects at all. Ranting against 17th century poets, pretty limited. What's best, though, is when your enemy is theirs, and they take *personal* joy in hearing you attack. Generic rants are best aimed at annoying people that just about everybody battles with in everyday life.

I have a few rants I've up-dated over years, changing out names and places, but keeping the basic subject and my complaints intact. These always work well and get Large Laughter. Here are three, abbreviated:

(1)

Women may not know this. They are certain men are idiots. But they may not know about this idiot behavior. Guys are standing at public restroom urinals next to each other, talking on their cell phones. You wouldn't have thought they had that kind of multi-tasking ability or dexterity, would you? So, that sound you hear when he's calling you isn't a fountain. For the record, if you can't even take a few minutes to pee in peace, it's not a sign you are *important*. It's a sign you're a moron.

(2)

I have a plan for balancing the budget and paying off the national debt, which I'll get to in a minute. So I'm second in line at the cash register at Kohls. Why? Because it is Sunday before I leave on a trip and I need socks and underwear. Guys do not buy underwear, incidentally, until they really *need* underwear. Women go buy underwear for special occasions or to perk up their mood or as a social activity. Men do not. So I need what I'm buying. I knew what I was after, went right to it, got it, and now I want to go. While the clerk I'm waiting for is waiting on the person in front of me, she is simultaneously carrying on a conversation with the clerk behind her about having to work an hour longer than she was supposed to and not getting her afternoon bathroom break and what an idiot the manager is – just like her boyfriend, who is also an idiot because. Taking twice as long as she would have had she been focused on the job, she gets that customer gone just seconds before blood starts squirting from my ears, and it is my turn. When her cell phone chirps and plays music and she answers and its her boyfriend who she is now talking to while muddling through the grudging act of waiting on me. So here's my plan for balancing the federal budget and paying off the national debt. Every so often there should be a week-long hunting season so you could buy permits to shoot people who talk on their cell phones when they're supposed to be waiting on you or when they're sitting right behind you in a restaurant. I should have shot her dead on the spot or better yet, saved the bullet and just used my gun or her phone and clubbed her to death right there – and any witnesses should have applauded. And it should be legal for me to do it. And if we have to buy permits to mete out this justice, fine, we'll buy them and gladly pay plenty, so that can wipe out the national debt.

Since the above two both involve cell phones, a piece of trivia: George Carlin used to do a rant about morons walking around attached to their Walkmans, with their headphones on all the time.

(3)

If you go to OfficeMax to buy anything, pack a lunch. I asked a clerk what I thought was a simple question. He is immediately talking into space. They all wear head-sets now and talk to each other, looking right at you but talking to an invisible someone else. Don't strangle them. They're helping you. So he's asking for help and quick as a bunny, another clerk arrives, who doesn't know anything either, so now they're both talking into the air, and with blinding speed, a third clerk arrives. And a fourth. And I'm surrounded. They're all talking to each other and maybe more hidden clerks - who knows? At this point, not only doesn't anybody know the answer, nobody even remembers the question. I can duck my head and quietly sneak out of the circle and they'll never notice. Go have lunch, roam around and finally find what I need, come back, and they'll still be there.

Chapter 17

PRANK HUMOR

ome years back, when Arab oil sheiks were gambling millions in Vegas, and buying up American companies, golf courses and blondes, a prank was pulled on the audience at a National Speakers Association convention. An Arab sheik in full regalia, gold-trimmed robe, head doohickey, pointy beard, was introduced as someone who had – in the previous week – bought up all the speakers bureaus and national trade associations in America. He then came on stage and very earnestly re-stated that and went on to tell the speakers that from now on, he would be deciding on their fees and whatever speakers were kept working would be working for him, serving at his pleasure. They would be required to assign all the copyrights to their books and tapes. And on and on. He was good and the dummies bought it. The room was silent, then buzz of whispering, then some people walking out, some stomping out, one yelling "Hell, no" – but most sitting, resigned to their fate, prepared to obediently curry favor from their new master. I'm pleased to say I got the gag in under 5 minutes and watched the whole thing, amused. They let it go for about 20 minutes before revealing the prank.

Some variation of this could easily be done at any association convention, industry boot camp, seminar, etc. – all you need is the premise and the "actor" capable of pulling it off.

This is the stuff all great publicity stunts and hokum pulled on public and media alike is made of, and if it interests you, you'll want to study P.T. Barnum, Houdini, and great publicity men like Bill Veck. Veck still remembered for inserting a midget into a major league baseball team's line-up, narrowing the strike zone to a square the size of a Tiffany's box.

Gary Halbert once had actor Ernie Borgnine's wife, Tova, hold a publicity-promoted event to "premiere" her new perfume, carrying the disclaimer, 'sworn under oath', that it 'contained no illegal sexual stimulants" despite the dangerous and amazing effects it seemed to have.

A number of comedians over years have gained massive media exposure by running mock-serious campaigns as presidential candidates. One of the comedians from The Smothers Brothers team, Pat Paulsen, did it. Twice. Much more recently, in outright theft from Paulsen, Stephen Colbert. A guy named John Kerry, too. Very funny.

Michael Moore is, incidentally, basically a P.T. Barnumesque promoter who relies heavily on stunts. The original movie that made him famous, *Roger & Me*, was a protracted stunt, Moore's pursuit, ambushing and ridicule of the then Chairman of General Motors. For his 2009 attack film *Capitalism*, the main commercial shows Moore with megaphone, on Wall Street, outside AIG's headquarters, hollering his intent to make a citizen's arrest – of the entire company. It's not as good as David Blaine's levitating in front of clustered passer-by on a busy street, but Moore levitating would require some very big, thick, impossible to conceal wires and a big orange crane.

Obviously, stunts have risk. Of falling flat, of being too easily seen through, or of working too well – like Orson Welles' original radio broadcast of *War of the Worlds*, which caused panic in the streets and got quite a few people injured. One of our Members, Chris Hurn, had one backfire and had to hurriedly issue retractions to the foolish media that had bit and reported his hokum as fact. Some years ago, when I was writing most of the ad copy for Joe Polish and his info-marketing business serving the carpet cleaning industry, I had deliberately made him into a pretty controversial figure, a lightning rod. I had him run a magazine cover showing himself costumed as Satan, standing back to back with himself as an angel, headline swiped from Glenn Turner: Con Man or Saint? My best brainstorm never got played out. I wanted to run an ad and send out press releases about Joe getting death threats due to his exposing the seedy underbelly of the business (cheap price bait 'n switch) and angering all his competitors who taught such antiquated and pathetic strategies. Have him photographed with his bodyguards. Joe feared it might actually encourage some nut to take a shot at him. I still like the gag, though, and you're free to borrow it if you like. With 20-20 hindsight, I wish I'd thought of it sooner and used it myself when I was doing a lot of marketing into the speaking industry. Attending an NSA convention with a team of bodyguards would have been fun.

I more recently created a stunt-gag I wanted to do at Glazer-Kennedy Insider's Circle™, but Bill vetoed it. To be fair, he'd have been cleaning up its mess not me. But we would have definitely gotten an accurate count on how many actually read my weekly faxes, sent to Diamond Members and above. Here's the fax I wanted to send:

SPECIAL **URGENT** FAX
FROM BILL GLAZER

April 1, 2008

DAN GONE MISSING !

I decided to tell you folks first – I'll be substituting for Dan in the weekly faxes and everything else, apparently from here on out. Follows, the note I received from Dan by Federal Express a few days ago. I have, of course, made many attempts to contact and locate Dan, to no avail. In Phoenix, Vicky reports receiving a large severance check and instructions to close the office and post no forwarding address. Of course, we all knew this day might come, but I certainly did not expect it to arrive so soon or abruptly, certainly not days before the SuperConference. I will obviously have to make an announcement about this at the SuperConference, and I would appreciate your support. Now here's Dan's letter:

Dear Members and Friends,

I've asked Bill to put this simple, brief letter in the newsletter and otherwise distribute it, presumably read it at the

SuperConference, as my most efficient way to say a very, very sincere THANK YOU and a GOOD-BYE to all of you.

On March 23, at 3:47 P.M., I hit my 'enough is enough number' and therefore <u>I quit</u>. Everything. As a matter of fact, I am gone. By the time this is public, homes will be up for sale, furnishings in storage, contracts terminated, phones disconnected, horses sold, and I will be invisible. I may be in Ireland. I may be in the Caribbean. But I won't be returning. I wish you all the very best of continued prosperity, and encourage you to continue working with Bill and his team. I apologize for missing the SuperConference, but as the saying goes, time waits for no man. I do have two new books coming out in May and June respectively, in the No B.S. series, and I hope you will enjoy them and profit from them, as my final contributions. (I have to promote *something*, even in this final missive.)

By the way, it might interest you that more than 50,000 people abruptly disappear every year, most never seen or heard from again. In many cases, they leave companies and families behind, everyone they know dumbfounded. They make no attempt to fake death or otherwise explain their disappearance. A few become news items, but most go unremarked upon. They are just gone. I've often wondered about these people. Now I am one.

Anyone with direct, pending business matters or projects in progress with me, will be hearing shortly from an attorney I've retained to close out my business affairs. Obviously, all consulting days, telephone appointments, Platinum meetings, etc. are cancelled. Please do <u>not</u> attempt to locate me. I have gone to extreme lengths to make that impossible, but would prefer not having my safeguards tested. I have no interest whatsoever in the world I have walked away from. It served me well and I feel that I have served it well, but it is past.

I have, incidentally, significantly altered my appearance, so any reported sightings of me will be false reports. The Internet will undoubtedly be abuzz with rumor-mongering. Please pay no attention. Focus on your business and your life, not my departure. And should you have concern for me, know that I am well, of sound mind, and happy. Just done.

Thank you again.

Sincerely,

Dan S. Kennedy

PS: There's a significant date at the top of this fax. April Fool's. Hey, the P.S. is the most important part of the letter. See ya in Nashville!

By the way, this day <u>will</u> come.

Which reminds me, I happen to believe Elvis has been alive for many years after his fake funeral. Whether he still is or not, I don't know. He'd be in his 80's. My theory is, he'd just had it, up and hit the road, and Priscilla and her gang quickly covered it up by faking his death, to keep his income production intact. He traveled around aimlessly for years, making money when he had to working in small town motel cocktail lounges as – an Elvis impersonator. I saw him myself, in the lounge at Tangiers in Akron, Ohio. Once he even brazenly entered a national Elvis impersonator contest in Vegas. Came in 3rd. My proof? Had he really been dead and buried, the entire country would have been consumed with a gigantic, catastrophic earthquake the day his daughter married Michael Jackson, caused by Elvis spinning in his grave. Anyway…

You *can* have a lot of fun with – and have your customers, readers or event attendees have fun being flummoxed by – a stunt or prank. You may, however, want to up your liability insurance.

Chapter 18

MISCELLANEOUS

- **How to tell an old joke:**

A dmit it. *This is an old joke you've probably heard, but it makes this point perfectly.* Work a few new lines or asides into it. If you're telling the ancient "must be a pony in here somewhere" story, still useful if doing 'motivation 101', and it still gets laughs – you can up-date the toys in the first room: an X-Box, Playstation 2, etc. Do NOT belabor it. Write it down and make it as short as it can be and still work.

- **How to tell a bad joke:**

Admit it. *Okay, this is a real groaner, and no self-respecting speaker would use it, but it makes this point perfectly.* Then sell it, hard; don't just lay it out there. At end, if they groan instead of laugh, say: *I told you so. It's a groaner. But the point…*

- **How to tell somebody else's joke:**

Credit the source. There are jokes or entire bits of material that literally belong to one person. Joan Rivers' first wife-second wife routine. Ron White's story of taking his dog Sluggo to the resort hotel. You can re-work his; it's impossible to use hers without anybody who is familiar with it recognizing it. The grayer area is with a story or joke that you know is not actually original or proprietary to somebody, but they use it a lot and there may be people in your audience who have heard that other speaker use it. Technically, it's anybody's stuff so it could be yours. But the risk of being thought of as a thief isn't worth taking. There's little downside to giving the credit. If you are going to switch it to first person and tell it as yours, you can handle it the way I do the cufflinks story: *I've heard a number of speakers tell their versions of this same story. It's a little reassuring to know that I'm not the only idiot. But here's how it happened to me...*

If you are following other speakers at a day-long or multi-day event, and you are not familiar with their material, you either need to be in there the whole time or ask the preceding speaker and/or host about specific jokes you intend using – *did anyone else tell the one about buying the bird at the bird store?*, or be extremely confident you are using truly original material. It's deadly to walk out and tell the same story a speaker before you told.

- **How to use somebody else's personal story:**

It's usually unwise to use anybody's truly proprietary story even with credit, but there are times when it actually does make a point better than any other, and its owner is famous and uses it. I re-tell Larry King's story about his gig M-C'ing a mob banquet in Miami. I tell the audience it's Larry's, tell it as Larry told it on the Success Events where we both spoke.

The bottom-line of all this is: don't steal. Sadly, our culture is more and more accepting of theft, and there is less and less respect for ownership of creative product. The internet generations outright advocate such theft, insisting that zero cost of delivery should mean zero cost of use, so they engage in theft of music, movies, print, business information, etc. with impunity. They have no understanding of disintegration of property rights – that what they engage in will circle around to them. In a society entirely made up of pirates, everybody must sleep atop their treasure with one eye open – not an easy trick if you wear an eye-patch. As an author, speaker and I dare say, entertainer, I *hate* thieves and pirates, and whenever I can, I punish them one way or another. Three kinds of punishment may befall you should you steal: first, being spotted by some in your audience, who think a lot less of you and may choose not to do business with you – and they may never voice their reasons. Two, a punch in the snoot, literally, or via lawyers. Copyright infringement, trademark infringement, even deliberate intent to create confusion in the marketplace for commercial advantage are *crimes*. The first two are felonies and they may very well bring the FBI to your door. One of my clients has, on three occasions, successfully involved the Feds in going after thieves of his DVD content. All may bring civil lawsuits, and involve actual and punitive damages. Third, karmic retribution in this lifetime or next or the one after that.

- **How to clean up a dirty joke:**

Same way you f***-a...make love to a porcupine. *Very carefully.* Many can be sufficiently cleansed to use, without castrating their effectiveness. Many cannot. Many are only funny dirty, some only funny filthy. If you are going to clean one up, you obviously have to take out the foulest or foul language and make the sex into 1950's euphemisms. At one time, movies had to cut away after the kiss and show trains going through tunnels or some such symbolic image. A Viagra® commercial that ran for a couple years still did the same thing: a man throwing a football through a tire. In sitcoms, only separate, single beds with the table with lamp between them allowed. This is how you have to think about a joke with sex in it.

So, here's an example of a cleaned up dirty joke, that is much funnier left dirty, but works okay, clean:

An elderly couple travel to the small town where they grew up and dated in high school, to celebrate their 50th wedding anniversary. They wander into the little main street diner and soda shop where they went on their first date for a late lunch. The owner waits on them, notices them holding hands, giggling. Overhears them low-talking. The husband asks the wife if she remembers sneaking out back, to the rear of the space behind the shop and, uh, doing the nasty there for the very first time. She does. They conspire. She goes to the back first as if going to the ladies' room, then out the door. He surreptitiously follows. After some time passes, since there are no other customers, the owner sneaks out to check on the lovebirds - and finds them in the back corner of the yard, she bent over holding onto the fence, he, pants around his ankles, also gripping the fence, the two *making love* frantically, *frantically,* until finally collapsing to the ground. The owner applauds. "I'm sorry for spying," he says, "but wow - at your age, you were making love like a couple of wild teenagers and I think that's terrific. Was it just like you remembered it?"

"Everything but the electrified fence. That's new."

I'll leave it up to you to reverse engineer it to the dirty version. Or, if you prefer, the dirtiest possible version for your own amusement. You could tell it this way to most audiences.

- **How to remember a joke:**

Punch line first, memorized precisely. You can usually re-construct backwards if you know the punch line. Writing them out by hand for your card file helps. Telling it to 7 to 10 people in quick succession helps. If you want to memorize a joke, story or entire speech, try 'sleep learning'. Record it perfectly on an endless loop cassette or multiple times filing a CD, hook the player to a pillow speaker and sleep on it. Seven nights in a row. With all that, though, use it or lose it still applies. I have more good, forgotten jokes than I do remembered jokes, and the less I speak and do long multi-day seminars providing opportunities to use them, the more fade away from memory.

- **How to improve a joke:**

Add detail, make it timely if you can use it in a timely way. And if appropriate, and you can get away with it, make it yours and tell it first-person. Consider these really weary, old gag lines about doctors:

It's not much of an HMO. If you break your leg, they've got a doctor who'll teach you how to limp. One time he treated a guy for 3ʳᵈ degree burns – turns out, the guy was an Indian. Tell him you feel funny, he tells you to go on TV.

You can imagine those in some very old stand-up. Bob Hope, maybe. Tweaked, Rodney Dangerfield. And, as a matter of fact, they come from joke-writers who worked for Hope and Dangerfield. But we could revive 'em today...

I've traveled to the future and returned to report. There, I had Obamacare. I broke my leg. My doctor taught me how to limp. While I was waiting, a guy came in complaining of pain all over his body. The doctor treated him for 3ʳᵈ degree burns. Didn't notice the poor guy was an Indian. I told my doc that I felt funny. He told me to go on America's Got Talent.

No, it's still not great stuff. But I made it 1ˢᵗ person and stuck in current references, and that helped it. *By the way, a couple other ways you know if you've got Obamacare: if the directions to the clinic include the words "turn left when you enter the trailer park"....if your pills are all different colors and have little M&M's on them....if your rectal exam is given by a nurse who looks suspiciously like Hillary Clinton – why, you might have Obamacare!*

• **How to change a joke:**

There's a wealth of old stuff that just can't be used anymore as it is, but can be re-purposed. This includes all the ethnic stuff. For example, this is an old joke about the Scotch, who were typecast as cheap and under-handed, this about a Scotsman sent to inform a good friend's widow of the poor sod's death. I've stripped the Scottish stuff out and made it over for degenerate gamblers. Found in any salesforce…

> So, every sales organization has its die-hard gamblers. Schemers, too, always trying to put one over on everybody. You've got one here. In this case, Billy, whose co-worker Charley Waters, had been accidentally run over by one of the installers' trucks and killed, drew the short straw and had to go and break the news to Mrs. Waters. He rang the doorbell and when she answered the door, asked "Is this Charley Waters' widow?"
>
> "I am his <u>wife</u>," she replied indignantly.
>
> "Sorry," Billy said. "How much would you care to bet on that?"

Hey, it's a death joke too – how 'bout that? Anyway, it's yanked right out of an old, old joke book. You might say it should be left there. But it works. I used it quite recently and got laughs.

There was a time, by the way, when Scots as cheapskates and cheats, and the Irish as drunks and brawlers were the subjects of hundreds and hundreds of jokes. Every immigrant group has been targeted in stereotype humor.

• LOL – Not:

There are times, much of the time, when you are using humor on stage that you want them laughing out loud. But it's far from necessary to serve most of our purposes. There is a distinction between comedy and humor. If doing comedy, you need LOL. If doing humor, you do not – they need only be *amused* by it, find it *pleasant*. When you tune into SNL and go the hour without laughing out loud a lot, you are disappointed, especially if you remember when it was Belushi, Aykroyd, Curtain, Murray and it was funny. If you listen to a recording or read a piece by Garrison Keillor, you may find it thoroughly enjoyable and entertaining and mood-lifting, yet never laugh out loud, and not be at all disappointed. No disrespect to Mr. Keillor intended.

This gets to the difference between a joke and a humorous story. A joke has a pretty simple structure, and is usually short. Often, just the set-up and the punch line. That term – PUNCH line – refers to boxing, the throwing of quick punches one after another. Often, a series of quick-punch jokes are strung together as a branded bit, like Foxworthy's *You Might Be A Redneck If....* Or Dangerfield's *I Don't Get No Respect* stuff. Jokes are usually about one big laugh. Load, punch. Laugh. A humorous story has a more complex structure, is richer in detail, develops, and should be built to get chuckles all along the way, building up to – and building the audience up to – the laugh at punch line. A seminar speaker definitely has the luxury of time to do this kind of material, and should. A stand-up comic usually does not.

If you listen to Charlie Jarvis tell the bird story, again and again and again, you'll have great demonstration of the chuckles-along-the-way strategy, used with that previous luxury of time. Charlie may be the best humorist ever to hang out with the National Speakers Association crowd.

But true stand-up is brutal. He got a shot with Carson. And got his head handed to him on a stick.

The secret of secrets is - timing. I understood it and learned it mostly by studying Johnny Carson and Charles Jarvis. Notwithstanding his disappointing outing on Carson, nobody has better timing as a humorous storyteller than Jarvis. I listened to Charlie's tapes until I wore them out, teaching myself timing. And here's the funny thing about timing: it's all about stops in the action, not about the action. Harry King defined timing as "knowing when to stop speaking in the midst of, in order to allow thinking time for the audience to catch up, to prepare itself for the laugh coming up, or to laugh." Further: "Stops, pauses, hesitations, grimaces and gestures are all tools for timing to allow what you've said to sink in to your audience's mind, so it can receive the punch line with receptive ear." The best way to turn an ordinary joke into a good, solid piece of material is with timing. If you just tell the "bring me my brown pants" leadership joke that's one thing; if you carefully draw out "bring – me – my –" and hesitate before saying "brown pants", it works 1,000 times better. And the build-up is far better told with timing than just written out on a page. My all-time favorite joke that requires timing and delay, so it doesn't work well on paper, is from inveterate gambler Walter Matthau:

I got a hot tip, went to the track, bet #3 in the third, named Bonanza's Coming – how could you go wrong? I got my binoculars and I watched that horse go around the track….and it was…*the*…*most*… *aggravating*… **30 minutes** of my life.

Chapter 19

ARE WE
HAVING FUN YET?

get asked this all the time: what, of all the things you do, do you *enjoy* most? Answer: not working at all. Do you *enjoy* being up there speaking? Answer: you can only enjoy it if you don't give a whit about any outcome.

Consider this, from Steve Martin:

"Enjoyment while performing was rare – enjoyment would have been an *indulgent* loss of focus that comedy cannot afford."

Further, in more gruesome detail:

"I stood on stage, blinded by the lights, looking into the blackness, which made every place the same. Darkness is essential: if light is thrown on the audience, they don't laugh. The audience necessarily remained a thing unseen except for a few front rows, where one sourpuss could send me into a panic and desperation. The comedian's slang for a successful show is: I murdered them. Which I'm sure came about because you finally realize the audience is capable of murdering you. ...... stand-up is seldom performed in ideal circumstances. Comedy's enemy is distraction, and rarely do comedians get a pristine performing environment. I worried about the sound system, ambient noise, hecklers, drunks, lighting, latecomers and loud talkers, not to mention the nagging concern 'is this funny?'..... I can remember instantly re-timing a punch line to fit around the crash of a dropped glass or raising my voice to cover a patron's ill-timed sneeze, seemingly microseconds before it happened."

Yep, if you're enjoying yourself up there, you're self-indulgent, at sacrifice of optimum effectiveness and results. And that's 10,000% truer if speaking – and using humor – to sell, rather than just entertain. "Fun" and "work" do not appear as synonyms in your thesaurus. For a reason.

I, too, fear and loathe audio-visual crews and technology. Even though I keep mine as simple as possible, I need it to function and – incredibly – few crews seem capable of meeting the most basic standard of competence: a microphone that stays on, has no crackle or feedback, tied to a sound system that can be heard clearly anywhere in the room, and a projector that projects. I, too, worry over the hecklers, the loud talkers, the ants-in-pants'ers who have to be up and down and in and out, the noise backstage or outside the room, the truly stupid who can't get the material, not to mention my own effectiveness: loss of voice, speed of speaking, forgetting a piece, getting the timing and inflection right, staying on schedule. I have had the ceiling crash in, the lights fail and the auditorium go black, the stage fill with swarms of flying bugs to swallow, the fire drill, the audience member keel over, a knife fight break out, etc. – and need to dodge, re-start, raise voice, re-capture attention, react in split-second. Better be concentrating and focused, focused, focused as if navigating unfamiliar ground loaded with land mines in the dark, in enemy territory. 'Cuz you are. Holding the audience's attention is a millisecond by millisecond matter. Distraction is not only the enemy of comedy, but the enemy of selling from the stage as well. So, no, I'm *not* enjoying myself up there, although I need to look as if I am. It *has to* look a lot easier 'n breezier than it is. I'm walking a tightrope 100-feet above an alligator infested pond. I'm wearing oversize, lead-weighted clown shoes. And I have vertigo. Fun? I don't think so.

Dean Martin was asked how he felt about his hit comedy-variety show, for which he famously refused to rehearse and was genuinely surprised by what went on during the show – and thus seemed to be having a helluva good time. He answered: "If it wasn't for having to do it, I'd like it just fine." When, five minutes in to an hour set, live on stage, he turned to his piano player, and audibly asked: "How long have I been up here?", he got laughter from the audience, but he might have been serious.

> *"It took me fifteen years to discover that I had no talent for writing, but I couldn't give it up because by that time I was too famous."*
>
> *- Robert Benchley*

Chapter 20

ARE YOU GOING TO
GET GOOD AT THIS?

In January 2009, I went, with a friend, to see Jerry Seinfeld at the Cleveland Playhouse. Because I'm in the Playhouse Donors Circle and have a good relationship with the Director of Donor Development, we had *very* front row, first row, at foot of stage, middle thus center stage seats. Looking right up at Jerry. Because of a blizzard and dysfunctional limo service, we were 20 minutes late. Very noticeably escorted to our seats by red-coated usher with flashlight. Jerry stopped, looked down, and asked, "Traffic?" Politely, gently, but pointedly. And an extra, free laugh.

Being this close to a stand-up comedian doing his thing, *this* close for only the second time in my life, I was very, very, very conscious of two things.

First, his nakedness. Of course he was *clothed*; grey tailored suit, white shirt, black tie, polished tie-top black dress shoes. But he was out there on a big, wide, deep black stage with a purple drape at its back, nothing else but stool with glass and bottle of water and microphone stand. Facing 1,000 people.

Most speakers have clutter. Have cover. Power-points presentations, a table with stuff, props. Zig has his pump, overheads. Rohn has his giant white board and markers. I have a table, a projector, stuff. There's signage. Sinatra said, "Any man who needs anything but a microphone and a spotlight is a putz." Try it the other way: any man willing to go out there for an hour or two with nothing but a microphone and a spotlight is a matador. A man of bravado and courage. There's no place to hide, nothing to help you, nothing to distract attention from you. It's not a presentation. It's a confrontation. It is the taking from the audience of what he wants.

He might as well have been naked.

A quarterback has some similarity, but there is cover. Was the interception his fault, a bad read, or his receiver's mistake....or a crosswind....? Maybe a baseball pitcher is more similar. He is naked on the mound. He has to throw with confidence. But he too has cover. An outfield to save him. A catcher calling for certain pitches. Maybe a golfer is even closer. But he's still not out there so blatantly naked. He has clubs, a caddie, the terrain. I don't think there's anything quite the same as this. Any performer in any field so vulnerable and fragile and at risk as this.

Watching Seinfeld work, I was very conscious of this because I so thoroughly understand it – and when working myself, strive not to think of it. It's said that right up to the very end, Carson still, every once in a while, vomited back-stage immediately before walking through those curtains to deliver the monologue.

Second, I was very aware that, because of that, as a necessity born of that, he exhibited unbridled certainty about his material. Not just confidence.

Certainty. And when I say "exhibited", I choose that word very deliberately. He puts it out there. It is in your face. He has come to have you laughing loud and long, so hard you cry, and you are going to do that. The couple times the intended audience response did not come he ignored it. He put his stuff across with zero hesitation, with forcefulness, with power. With Seinfeld, there is, of course, seasoning, experience, exceptional ability and talent at writing material, and the benefit of fame; the presumption by the audience that he is supposed to be funny, so he is. I was also seeing a meticulously crafted, timed, practiced and practiced and practiced routine. He has an interesting choreography trick, a way of telling the audience a piece of material has ended and applause is in order – that's when he stops, and turns his back – courageous itself – to walk to the stool and sip water. The audience gets it. They applaud at each water break. He is in total control up there.

Naked before 1,000 of us and still in total control. That ain't easy.

And that's what I was reminded of, more than anything else. **Mastery ain't easy.**

Yes, he had some very good material, some old, some new. But some of the material was pretty common and pedestrian too. He did a bit about the Cialis ads with the two bathtubs, and threw in lines about "if your erection lasts longer than four hours" – something every comedian has used and uses. His little routine about golf wasn't even half as good as my bit about golf. His bit about Starbucks better than mine. But the material is a relatively small part of this game. It's putting it across that matters most. You could furnish the same material to any number of other comics and a lot of speakers and they'd die up there with it. Lots of folks can deliver a presentation. Many can be funny. But taking total and complete control and holding it, keeping it the entire time you're out there, only releasing it after you've exited, well, that's something not many people can do. They *could*. If they set out to master it and invested all that is required to achieve that mastery.

> *"Nobody realizes that*
> ***I work eighteen hours a day**
> *for a solid month to*
> *make that hour of TV*
> *look like it's never been rehearsed."*
>
> *- Jimmy Durante*

So it is with everything. Mastery of anything is, I think, possible by just about anybody. But it ain't easy. Or quick.

In his book *Born Standing Up*, comedian Steve Martin explained it this way: **"I did stand-up comedy for 18 years. Ten of those years were spent learning, four years spent refining, and four years spent in wild success."** He began working as a bit performer in stage shows at Disneyland. He became the #1 comedian-concert performer, filling stadiums as if a rock band. And there you have it. Personally, it's taken me about ten years to get all-pro, peak performing, top-shelf good at anything and everything. If I start something new, I know I need to be prepared for that kind of haul. And at my age, I'm not casting about for anything new to start. I don't even want to risk *watching* golf.

Of course, there's no need for you to get really good at comedy, if you aren't or don't aspire to be either a frequently working professional speaker/

platform salesperson, influential writer, direct-response copywriter or, God help you, an actual comedian. If you need to do a little of some of these things, only occasionally, and get to work in environments and situations not demanding truly professional competence, you can skate by with something much less – and much of this book is devoted to helping you do just that. Nothing wrong with it. Just be conscious of your decisions. Don't pretend or con yourself that you are serious about mastering something when you aren't. Don't foolishly underestimate the difficulty of this or any other craft, either. Be honest about it, know your limitations, and act accordingly.

One favor, don't insult those of us who are dedicated, serious, heavily invested professionals at this – or at anything else – by acting as if you can nap through one weekend seminar or skim a couple books and then join us *as peers*. It's insulting to us and it makes you seem a moron. That's why I was never angry at the very cold shoulder I got from most of the professional harness racing drivers when I first started driving. The idea of a guy my age, by their perception dropping down out of the luxury seats in the clubhouse, climbing into the sulky and acting as if he could go with them was an insult. I got it. I fought past it and earned respect. Paul Newman had exactly the same experience as a race car driver. He understood it too. This does not mean you should genuflect and grovel for decades when any pro or master passes by. It's not that simple. Any top pro who needs that is as big an ass as the amateur who thinks he's a pro. Just be respectful of the craft itself, those who've paid high price to master it, those who have history with it.

Whatever you do, try not to take comedy for granted.

Chapter 21

MAKE 'EM LAUGH & TAKE THEIR MONEY

It was suggested to me that using this as this book's title would be "off-putting" to some people. Perhaps in the same sort of way that Robert Ringer's original title, *Winning Through Intimidation,* was off-putting, and criticized by reviewers (who probably never read the book). Its newest edition bears the slightly gentler title *To Be Or Not To Be Intimidated?* Intimidation is a subject, like manipulation, like power, that disturbs many people. They are unclear of their motives and uncomfortable with their pursuit of success, so they are very uncomfortable with anybody who is very clear about it.

The straightforward, direct determination to make money in general, and in this case, to turn an audience upside down and empty its pockets, is very unsettling to a lot of people.

So it was suggested I might *not* want to be so clear about the motives that have driven my business life, my choices of study and skill development, my speaking and my use of humor.

The suggestion was *not* well received.

Vincent Palko
www.AdToons.com

One of the main reasons I like the title so much is that it will make a lot of people mad. Or decide they don't like me. And decide not to read the book. I enjoy *rattling* people. It's fun to push their buttons. And a very easy button to push is peoples' desperate need to deny self-interest. Another, their tortured relationship with money.

You might think I'm being tongue-in-cheek. You might prefer thinking that. Permit me to destroy that nice notion.

Seems to me there's an over-abundance of Oprah-ized, stroller pushing, hyper sensitive half-men, scared-silly politically correct tip-toeing mamby-pampbys, and very, very confused folks – men and women - without requiring my participation. They can all join hands in a sensitivity circle and recite poetry to each other if that'll make 'em happy. Or talk about how offensive I am, if that'll make 'em even happier. If I can be of service without losing skin off my nose, I'm here to please. In 30 years at this, I've given a lot of people a lot of happiness by giving them somebody to gossip about, criticize, dislike. I only regret that they get to do that for free.

Personally, I prefer dealing with people who are very clear about what they're about and where they stand, no mystery, no equivocation. Consider the Akmajanidofus guy running Iran. As of this writing, he has flat-out stated he believes the holocaust never occurred but that he intends to remedy that, his purpose is to wipe Israel off the globe, and he's hustling to amass enough nuclear capability to do it. Were I in charge, I would know exactly how to deal with him. Obama thinks the appropriate course of action is treating him as a personal pen pal and hopefully sitting down soon, one on one, and chatting with him. I have a different thought. I'd rather deal with Akmawhatshisface than with Obama, by the way. Obama's all about concealing and disguising what he's about. The midget Hitler running Iran has a lot more *integrity*.

"These are my principles.
If you don't like them
I have others."

- Groucho Marx

My number one reason for being such a fan of Ronald Reagan was his clarity, transparency and forthrightness about who he was and what he was about. When Reagan told the air traffic controllers they had to be back to work on Monday or all be fired, everybody thought he was bluffing. He wasn't. Lots of people think he *accidentally* left his mike on when he talked about pushing the button. I think he was deliberately sending a message. Gorbachev did not think he was bluffing.

So I'm always clear as glass just wiped down with Windex®. **I'm here for the money**. If it weren't for the money here, I'd be somewhere else. So, don't flatter yourself, ever.

I make no apologies. I do exert enormous effort to provide value meaningful to those whose pockets I'm attempting to empty. But I do not apologize for my purpose. To borrow from Zig, my attitude is that you have *my* money in your pocket and it is up to me to fix that little error. If your laughter allows me to get what I'm after, that's my motivation to be such a serious student of comedy.

So, about the title. People who feel need to apologize for total dedication to and aggressive pursuit of their own self-interest and I are not in harmony, never will be, so why entice them past a book's cover only to have them horrified a few pages in? I feel sorry for such people. I can't imagine the deep, private pain of going through life feeling like you ought to be apologizing for your ambition. How sad. But as sorry as I may feel for such confused souls, I don't want to attract them.

"Comedy is very controlling – you are making people laugh.
It is there in the phrase; making people laugh."

- Gilda Radner

Mental fog, confusion, timidity have no place in making money. In speaking. In comedy. Its polar opposite, absolute clarity of purpose is everything. The successful stand-up comic is very clear about going out there and *making them* laugh. Not necessarily liking him. Laughing. The speaker using humor as a tool must have one absolutely clear purpose for his use of all his tools: going out there and getting their money. Either speak to sell or don't, but if you choose – or need to choose the former, don't be half-pregnant about it, embarrassed about it, apologetic about it, emotionally conflicted about it. They'll *smell* that. They'll eat you alive. Specific to speaking, my advice is – if you're conflicted about your purpose – stay off the stage. Going out there's going to make you miserable.

By the way, a lot of people do what they do because they want or need to effect transfer of other peoples' money to them. In fact, that's why most people do most things. But they prefer personal delusion and perpetuated illusion that other things are more important to them. Really? So who among them is working for free? I just annoy these panty-waists because I don't feel any need to disguise my motives, and they do, and they secretly wish they didn't. By the way, guess who I want as a waiter or waitress? The one who is absolutely clear about his or her ambition to end the shift with the biggest bucket of tips possible. That's who will give me the best service, the best experience. I don't want some half-committed, unsure, Michael Moore influenced, socialist leaning schlump who thinks all tips ought to be divided evenly. From her, I'll never get a second cup of coffee. Same principle is true with everything. Choose the cardiac surgeon most concerned with his own career and reputation and wealth. Read the book written by the guy who is all about getting you hooked on him so you'll buy more books.

Well, I hope you enjoyed this book. I prefer you get value from it than not. If you send me a letter of praise or a report of using something from it to fatten your bank account or otherwise add joy or skill or accomplishment to your life, I'll read it and derive some satisfaction from it. But all that is just *gravy*. And I can get along very nicely without any of that, too. I wrote this because the subject interests me and I'm a serious student of it and think I have interesting things to say about it, so, to some extent, I wrote it for myself. But I never would have written it just to indulge my own interests. Let there be no doubt. My *main* purpose in writing this was to wind up with something I could exchange for *your* money.

Louis L'Amour, the legendary writer of countless western novels, was grinding them out in days when publishers didn't pay royalties. Writers were paid once. He was asked why all his heroes fired all the bullets in their guns, why *everybody* died from six shots, never one. He replied, "Because I get paid by the word." So much for creative, artistic integrity.

EPILOGUE

Maybe The Advice-Giving Business Isnmt Such A Good Business After All

So, another book of advice under my belt. I've been in the advice-giving business since long before I had any right to dispense any. I have only recently begun thinking I might have made any number of better choices. One of the biggest advice givers of all time was Socrates. And they poisoned him. We all know what happened to that loudmouth carpenter. Way too preachy.

Giving advice – or selling it – and having it ignored is frustrating. The more you're paid for it the less that happens, and the less frustrating it is when it does. I assure you, being paid $2,000.00 an hour to be ignored is less aggravating than being paid $200.00 and ignored. Money is soothing balm. I think if I could find somebody who'd pay me a paltry $200,000.00 a month to occasionally solicit and steadfastly ignore all my advice, I could finally be a happy man. Relax under the banyan tree with a good book. Of course, there's nothing more futile than dispensing *free* advice – other than dispensing free advice to a family member.

Seems like it's a little less taxing to just be funny. As I look back, I think I coulda been a contenda. Letterman, for example, came from the same small-town midwest I did. He showed a little flair as a stand-up comic, was spotted and snagged by a woman who became his chief joke-writer and producer, got mentored by Leno, nearly adopted by Carson (made a guest host after four appearances), and fine-tuned a persona as a grumpy, sarcastic smart-ass. I could do *that*. It took him all the way to the very top of the comedy/entertainment world: his very own, very public sex scandal.

Just like the V-8 commercial. Smack myself in the head and say: I could've had *that* career.

Do you ever have such thoughts? Of course you do. Everybody ponders greener pastures and might-have-been's. Maybe, maybe Gene Simmons doesn't. Everybody else does. Would I take Letterman's or Limbaugh's chair? In a New York minute with time left over. But, like so many people feel about their pipe-dreams, only if it was offered. *Not* if I have to go earn it. At this point, I'm fairly certain the career I have is the career I'll finish with, the two of us limping off into the sunset together, hopefully before we are thrown out.

Anyway, this book has not been about really serious, really deep, really profound advice. Most speakers and writers just need and want to be a little bit funnier, and I think we made it over that low bar. Mike Vance titled one of his books *Raise The Bar*, and when I first saw it, I thought: there's a mis-judgment of the market. A much more easily embraced idea, the title of a bestseller: *Don't Sweat The Small Stuff*. Essentially, lower the bar. Hey, we're doing it with schools, SAT's and college admissions, entry to the military, movies, TV and music, news media, even language and communication – from actual words and sentences to text abbreviations and tweets to, soon, certainly, just grunts – so why not with comedy? Heck, if you're cheating and skimming this first, just read Chapter 7 about Cheating, and be done with it.

> *"He wrote to tell me that I wasn't funny.*
> *I wrote back to tell him there was a difference*
> *between him not being amused*
> *and me not being funny."*
>
> *- Dan Kennedy*

Now you sense my growing frustration with being an advice-giver, causing my re-thinking of my career. The longer I'm at it, the more I find myself offering up unwelcome advice, too lengthy and complex advice. To swipe and paraphrase, there's a rapidly shrinking market for thoughtful truth. The desire for messages limited to 146 characters makes we wish I hadn't skipped out on class the day they learned haiku. I have yet, however, encountered any reason to regret exiting with no understanding whatsoever of algebra. By the way, in high school, I briefly had the hots for a girl named Malu Halasa. Hadn't thought of her once in all this time. The words 'haiku' and 'algebra' popped her into my head. My mind works in mysterious ways.

And I guess that's the upshot of it all, advice-giving, or writing, or speaking, or comedy. At its core, it's about how your mind works. *If* your mind works. Quite a few folks let theirs retire very early. If your mind thinks in terms of solutions, advice-giving may be just the right thing for you. If your mind finds funny in everything – especially things others do not find funny, comedy may be just the ticket. Your mind is trainable and can be conditioned to focus on whatever you want it to focus on. This is important, given the wise adage that "we become what we think about most." The oldest joke about that is, if it's true, most men would be either vaginas or ham sandwiches.

Anyway, despite the commercial worthlessness of doing so, I hope this book made you think and makes you think. That is, as playwright Archibald MacLeish noted, the only thing that really separates men from pigs. Thought rather than simple instinct.

I welcome your thoughts, should you care to share them.

Fax 602-269-3113.

"I doubt that a children's book about beer would sell."

© Frank Cotham/Condé Nast Publications/www.cartoonbank.com.

RESOURCES

This is NOT meant as a complete or exhaustive list - rather a beginning. It includes a sampling of some of the reference books in my work-library, and the comedians and humorous writers I've paid and pay most attention to. It omits more than it includes, however. Although all are important, I've marked the bare-minimum essentials with an asterisk(*).

Required References & Joke Swipe FIles

Esar's Comic Encyclopedia* - Evan Esar

2500 Jokes For All Occasions - Moulton

2400 Jokes To Brighten Your Speeches - Robert Orben

5600 Jokes For All Occasions - Meiers/Knapp

Milton Berle Joke File - Milton Berle

Treasury of American Humor - Gene Shalit

Readers Digest's Collection of: Laughter Is The Best Medicine

Prairie Home Companion Pretty Good Jokebook

Funny Bone - Dr. Herb True

"I bet on a horse at 10-1.

It didn't come in until half past five.

- Henny Youngman

Quote Books

Mark My Words* - Nigel Rees

Don't Squat With Yer Spurs On - Texas Bix Bender

"Love conquers all.

Except poverty and a toothache."

- Mae West

Business Humor

The Dilbert Principle - Scott Adams

New Yorker Book of Business Cartoons

Sun Tzu Was A Sissy - Stanley Bing

***All books and essays* by Stanley Bing**

"Anyone can do any amount of work,

provided it isn't the work

he is supposed to be doing at that moment."

- Robert Benchley

How-To Books

How To Be A Comedian For Fun & Profit – by King/Laufer
(This is the very first book I ever got about how to do comedy. I have it still, all marked up with an orange-colored hi-liter pen.)

Great Comedians' Books

I Had The Right To Remain Silent – But I Didn't Have The Ability – Ron White
Brain Droppings – George Carlin
Cosbyology - Bill Cosby
Born Standing Up - Steve Martin
Me Of Little Faith - Lewis Black
Without Feathers - Woody Allen

Books About Comedy

I'm Dying Up Here – W. Knoedelseder
Bob Hope: A Life In Comedy - William Faith
Make 'Em Laugh - The Funny Business of America* (Book &/or DVD)

Humorous Writing

Of All Things* - Robert Benchley

Money Secrets* - Dave Barry

All other books, columns, essays by Dave Barry

All books, columns, essays by Nora Ephron

All books, columns, essays by Erma Bombeck

Driving Like Crazy* - P.J. O'Rourke

America - John Stewart & The Daily Show

Semi-Tough - Dan Jenkins (a novel)

Life Its Ownself - Dan Jenkins (a novel)

Novels by Carl Hiassen

Novels by Elmore Leonard

Anthology of Humor Writing from *The New Yorker** - David Rennick

The Most of Andy Rooney - Andy Rooney

P.S. Your Cat Is Dead* - James Kirkwood

Humor In Advertising

$ellebrity* - George Lois

Outrageous Advertising That's Outrageously Successful* – Bill Glazer

MADvertising – David Shayne

Art of Selling Using Cartoons - Vince Palko

There's A Customer Born Every Minute (About P.T. Barnum)* - Joe Vitale

Misc.

Gorgeous George - John Caponya

Sex, Money, Kiss - Gene Simmons

King of Madison Avenue - Roman

When TV Was Young - Ed McMahon

Here's Johnny - Ed McMahon

ALL MY BOOKS. All of them. Every single one.

AUDIO PROGRAMS

The Humor Workshop* - Dr. Charles Jarvis

Everything you can find by Dr. Charles Jarvis

Something Like This: The Bob Newhart Anthology* - Bob Newhart

GLAZER-KENNEDY RESOURCES

(At www.DanKennedy.com or call 410-825-8600)

Dan Kennedy's INFLUENTIAL WRITING Workshop

How To Create Personality in Copy/Customers for Life - Dan Kennedy

Dan Kennedy's POWER POINTS (Manual & Searchable CD)

Dan Kennedy's Creative Thinking for Entrepreneurs Workshop

Big Mouth, Big Money - Dan Kennedy

(d'ya see a pattern here?)

APPENDIX 1

Selected political columns by Dan Kennedy from those published regularly by BusinessAndMedia.org, associated with the Media Research Center in Washington D.C.

Environmental Sensitivity Notice

This book is Certified 100% Green. It is printed on paper made exclusively from very old trees with chronic diseases, that toppled over of their own accord and passed away from natural causes. Before transport to the saw mill powered entirely by ethanol and Ed Begley Jr. pedaling his stationary bicycle, any remaining leaves were meticulously plucked by hand and chopped into nutritious salad mix, bagged in re-useable hemp bags (not plastic), and shipped to third-world countries to provide vitally needed meals for the starving. Any insects or small woodland creatures living in the trees were carefully removed and gently released into the wild. Should you tire of the book and decide not to make it a permanent resident in your library, please responsibly recycle. The pages will be a bit scratchy, but you can take comfort in doing your duty as a citizen of Spaceship

Earth. If you meet Sheryl Crow on the road, proudly tell her you used only one page each time. THIS is what it means to be an American.

Inspirational Quotation

"We are just going to have to learn that we can no longer drive the cars we want, drive wherever we want to, eat as much food as we feel like eating, and keep our houses' thermostats set at 72 degrees."

- Barack Obama

Finally, Good News About The Economy

ECONOMIC NATURAL SELECTION WOULD DOOM LAWYERS, CONGRESS AND OTHER 'NON-ESSENTIAL' ENTITIES.

By Dan Kennedy

Business & Media Institute

2/11/2009 11:41:23 AM

THE JANUARY 26TH ISSUE OF "The Wall Street Journal" finally provided some really cheery news about the economy with the joyful headline: "Recession Batters Law Firms, Triggering Layoffs, Closings."

I've long advocated a government imposed one- to two-generation moratorium on lawyers breeding. It would certainly have the support of the vast majority of Americans, but it would raise some thorny ethical and legal issues. So this is the next best thing: a Darwinian thinning of the one herd that probably takes more from the economy than any other, and contributes little. Cannibals even refuse to eat lawyers. It leaves a bad taste in their mouths.

The article says layoffs at law firms are now "commonplace." Wonderful. Is there any other population of workers in this economy that could be furloughed en-masse and do less harm by its shrinkage?

Yes, actually there is – Congress, which, not coincidentally, has a lot of lawyers in its ranks. If only we could lay off Congress for two or three years. If they're all home collecting extended unemployment compensation, doing nothing, none of their legislation – or the president's – can move. And the country will be better off.

After all, most of the blowhards now arguing over how to best spend a trillion or more to solve our economy's ills are the same incompetents and bought-and-owned toadies who drove it off the cliff in the first place. Having Barney Frank and Chris Dodd engineering the repair of the banking system is like putting the navigator from the Titanic in charge of your cruise.

Every bit of meddling and blindfolded spending Congress has done so far has, by every possible measurement, made things worse, and there's every reason to assume their next bumbling move will too. They are, at best, Inspector Clouseaus. Less charitable interpretations are easily justified. Either way, it's impossible to imagine us winding up worse off if the whole bunch of them went on extended vacations.

Here's a parallel for someone in the media to draw, if they care to: Members of Congress now bitterly complain that they voted for TARP #1 based on false information about a ginned up crisis. Just like they insist the Bush Administration sold them the Iraq War. And just like they're now cooperating with their new president in selling both TARP #2 plus another 800-billion dollars or so of spending. Are they fools who can be easily, repeatedly fooled by the same trick, or co-conspirators in repetitive fraud? Either way, their absence would put the brakes on the headlong trebling of the accumulated debt, and that would be a good thing.

In Washington D.C., when it snows, the news broadcasts carry the government's notice to all non-essential government workers to stay home. In a rare bit of honesty on its part, Congress usually does take those days off. In California now, in honor of its budget crisis, Arnold has ordered all non-essential government employees to take two days off each month without pay. If they're non-essential, why are they there at all? In small business, we have no non-essential employees. Only the essential ones.

There is that Shakespeare quote: first, kill all the lawyers. And it must feel like death for them to get pink slips and the suggestion that they try their hand at earning honest livings. The economy is expanding these terminations to everyone and everything non-essential. It is right, and those trying to stop this shedding of its dead skin, wrong.

So, here's what we do: cut all the non-essential spending that cannot be proven beyond shadow of doubt to be a stimulant from the stimulus package. Let all the non-essential employees in every place have their jobs eliminated, and let them make themselves essential somewhere else, doing essential work. Let the failed, functionally bankrupt companies disappear and we'll discover none were essential. Let the economy cleanse itself of all the non-essential sludge and re-birth itself, shiny and new.

Stimulus and Spending: Synonyms Not

SOMEONE GET THE LEADER OF THE FREE WORLD AND HIS MEDIA PALS A THESAURUS.

By Dan Kennedy

Business & Media Institute

2/18/2009 10:06:01 AM

LAST WEEK, PRESIDENT OBAMA EXPLAINED as if talking to the dim-witted that stimulus is synonymous with spending. The fawning media swallowed it whole and regurgitated it as gospel.

While I did not go to Harvard, I do own a dictionary. Several, in fact, as well as a thesaurus, the dictionary of synonyms. And I have consulted them. It turns out my initial thought about this was right and the president is incorrect.

No surprise there, given Obama's evermore visible difficulty with separating fact from fiction. Take, for example, his assertion during a speech at Caterpillar that passage of his spending package would enable the earth-mover maker to immediately re-hire many of its laid off workers. The CEO of the company instantly corrected him. The yet unproven success of Obama's package plus other stimulus spending by other governments around the world should enable the re-creation of some of these jobs over time, he explained. But for now, passage or no passage, he was laying off another umpteen thousand workers.

So, the facts about stimulus and spending: synonyms not.

My thesaurus lists a dozen synonyms for stimulus; none are spend.

According to The American Heritage Dictionary, 'spend' means to use up, to pay out, to wear out, exhaust, *waste, squander.* The dictionary doesn't have a definition for spending with money you don't have – say a trillion dollars, on which you will owe billions of dollars you don't have of interest to China, so you'll later need to borrow more and go deeper in debt just to pay the interest. To get this, you'd have to match its definition of "spend" with its definition of "stupid."

The Dictionary does have a definition for "stimulus," though, and guess what? The word "spend" doesn't appear there! A "stimulus" is defined as something that stimulates; *an incentive.* Fitting that definition nicely would be, as example, new incentives to investors to step in and purchase real estate in foreclosure, in quantity. Or new incentives to consumers to buy automobiles and houses. Or new incentives to business owners to risk, expand, hire. Fitting this definition nicely might be capital gains tax cuts or waivers (not increases or threats of increase), income tax cuts for those most able to invest significantly (not increases or threats of increases).

Not fitting this definition of "stimulus" at all is pouring billions of borrowed dollars to later be repaid by taxpayers (and the cruelest tax on lower income earners: rampant inflation) into protecting mice in San Francisco, extra support for the National Endowment of the Arts, school construction in areas with declining enrollments, or gifts to criminally irresponsible home buyers. The definition doesn't even include handing big bundles of cash to state governors to merely duct tape over their budget holes from the spending they've already done. The only thing being stimulated by this spending is the blood pressure of those of us who'll be compelled to pay for it.

In his defense, the media has told us that the new president is so busy and besieged with urgent work – like flying around the country for photo ops and speeches – that he hasn't yet had time to unpack all his boxes and get his office organized. Maybe his dictionary is still tucked away in an unpacked box.

If you have a friend in mainstream media, you know what to get them next Christmas, if there is a Christmas. A dictionary and a thesaurus.

Mr. President, Oprah's got the Right Idea

A MODEST PROPOSAL FOR THE DETROIT DEBTORS.

By Dan Kennedy

Business & Media Institute

2/25/2009 10:17:37 AM

WE KNOW THEY'RE CHUMMY. We know she knows cars – she's given them to every member of her audience before. So why shouldn't President Obama install his pal Oprah as the new federal Car Czar and let her run one more government giveaway lollapalooza?

Let's not kid around. We are going to give GM unlimited numbers of billions of dollars to keep its UAW workers employed until they voluntarily retire with those "golden parachute" buy-outs that so offend Obama when executives get them.

So let's just *buy* cars. Buy all the cars they can make. Have GM stop making anything but that cute little golf cart they're calling the Volt, and buy millions of 'em every year. Make every elected official, all government bureaucrats and field agents drive them. Every CEO of a company getting bail-out money, too. Oprah can give one free to everybody who buys a house in foreclosure – with the gifting done to crowds in stadiums, televised live, every night. The messiah loves crowds in stadiums.

But why stop there? Have her hand them out as freebies to *everybody* making less than some decided-upon income ... it does sound vaguely familiar, doesn't it? A chicken in every pot, a car in every garage.

Hang 'em from trees on the White House lawn and let the little kiddies get them during the Easter car hunt. Barter them for world peace: Obama can sit down for tea with vile dictators and give them Chevys in exchange for promises not to attack our embassies, ships, citizens or buildings. Park a bunch of them outside San Francisco and let those endangered little mice Pelosi's so worried about live in them. In fact, make some without wheels to give out as home-pods for the homeless. If they'll cut holes in these things' roofs, they can be sold as Christmas tree stands; stick the tree through the roof, plug the lights into the dashboard, plug the car into the wall socket. Make the headlights flash and horn beep to the tune of "Santas's Coming to Town" with the remote. Appropriate 'cuz Santa has come to Washington.

The hardest thing to swallow about Santa is the idea he can deliver toys to every home in just one night. But when you see just how much money President Obama's been able to throw around in just 30-odd days, you begin to think anything's possible.

One big difference: the real Santa makes the toys he gives away – and actually does create jobs, for elves and reindeer. Santabama pays for the toys he gives away with money he steals from you and me. He creates nothing. He is a bigger thief than Madoff times 10,000. And an even bigger con artist. He is no more interested in economic recovery or stimulus or, for that matter, fairness than O.J. has been in finding the real killer. He is about socialist consolidation of power, nothing more, nothing less. Unless he's just an imbecile, which I don't think anyone would accuse him of.

Back to the auto industry mess. With very, very, rare exceptions, the media reports on and pundits discuss this evolving scandal with the premise accepted that if we lose these two car companies – GM and Chrysler – we lose the auto industry in toto. On a Sunday morning talkfest this past weekend, the governor of Michigan plaintively squealed at a counterpart from another state that he apparently wants to live in a country that makes *nothing*. But the other governor is from a state with a factory making cars, owned by a company that isn't bankrupt.

This premise is dunderheaded. Why does the media insist on presenting it as reality? There once were something like 2,000 American car-makers. There was once a Big 4. The fourth, American Motors, came from Rambler, which came from Nash, and which handed Jeep over to Chrysler. American Motors' failure did not end auto-making or all other manufacture here. Nor would GM's. Americans will buy about 8-million new cars in 2009. Somebody's going to make them and well-run companies can and will compete for that business. And these cars won't all come from a workshop in Samoa, in kits sold in boxes at IKEA stores.

Failed companies are supposed to fail and disappear. Airlines have gone; there are still airlines. It is just not the role of government to use taxpayers' money to interfere. When government picks which privately owned enterprises to prop up and which not to, those decisions never get made for business reasons; they're made for *political* reasons. They punish well-run companies by funding failing or failed companies, grossly distorting economic reality. They do this, they say, in order to preserve jobs. But in truth those jobs would move, not disappear. It's disgraceful that the media accepts this faulty, fraudulent premise and sells it to the public.

One more job left for Oprah. There's that huge inventory of unsold, politically objectionable, gas guzzling Hummers. Who can she give those to?

Big Government in an Itsy Bitsy, Teeny Weeny Bikini

THE NANNY STATE WAXES HUGE.

By Dan Kennedy

Business & Media Institute

4/1/2009 10:28:49 AM

AN ENTIRE WEEKLY NATIONAL MAGAZINE could be devoted just to tracking government interference, regulations, new regulations, pending regulations and regulations threatened just to bring forth competing lobbyists with money. Anybody who would insist any business or industry is "unregulated" is a liar of grand proportions.

Because of my work, I receive and read trade journals from more than 50 different industries and fields. Every one devotes pages every month to new government meddling.

But the general public doesn't read industry trade journals. They don't read Nation's Restaurant News, to see that just as the trans-fat ban has taken hold, the next wave – regulation of restaurants' use of sodium (salt) – is on the horizon. They don't read the Farm Bureau publications to hear of changes in federal guidelines for beekeeping. They don't read the direct marketing publications' reporting on do-not-mail list legislation percolating in a dozen states (somewhat similar to do-not-call, threatening to increase the USPS' deficits, kill jobs at USPS and throughout the private sector, hamper small businesses and give advantage to colossal ones.)

So. The New Jersey Board of Cosmetology and Hairstyling has most recently been applying its bureaucratic, regulatory zeal to one of the state's biggest crises: injuries sustained by women seeking the perfect bikini line. Apparently, two – count 'em now, *two* – women have been hospitalized for infections purportedly resulting from getting Brazilian bikini waxes that completely bare the genitals. One has even sued, according to the spokesman for New Jersey's Division of Consumer Affairs, the government agency that oversees the other government agency, the Board of Cosmetology and Hairstyling. I didn't get this from local media in New Jersey, by the way. It was picked up as news of such national importance it made its way across states, to the D.C. Examiner, a Washington, D.C. newspaper.

I seem to recall much bigger numbers of people taken deathly ill by lead poisoning in everything from toys to toothpaste to foods imported from China, that we lack the financial resources and manpower to police. Thousands are apparently destitute thanks to losses with Madoff, AIG, Fannie Mae and Freddie Mac, General Motors and other long-running financial scams perpetrated right under the noses of regulators and Congress.

On Meet The Press, Arizona Senator John McCain blandly acknowledged that his home city, Phoenix, was now 'the kidnapping capitol;' a kidnapping a day in Phoenix – U.S. citizens dragged across the Mexican border we lack the will and resources to control. He didn't express outrage or put forth an urgent plan for this crisis.

It's actually kind of cheery to think of a place with so few problems its government is free to focus on dangerous bikini waxing. Maybe we should all move to the Garden State.

Seriously, this sort of thing is representative of everything that's wrong with the idea of government as parent. Trying to take enough tax dollars from us to fund mammoth bureaucracies to interfere with and micro-micro-manage every little detail of everyone's lives, largely by piling impossible regulation on top of impossible regulation on every business, large and small. To paraphrase the enraged CNBC reporter's screamed question about mortgage bail-outs, do you really think *you* should be paying to make bikini waxing safe for the women of your city, state or the country? Is this what you have in mind when you watch from one-third to three-fourths of your income swallowed up by government? Which do you judge more critical: more cops on the streets or more cosmetology inspectors in bikini wax salons?

We really must grow up, before the cost of government as parent crushes us all to death.

As silly as my chosen example is – intended to let you make up your own jokes – it is symbolic of the great war we now find ourselves in. On one side are those determined to build an all-seeing, all-knowing, all-doing, cradle-to-grave parental bureaucracy that invades even the most trivial aspects of our lives with promises of no individual risk and no personal responsibility at whatever impossible cost. On the other side are those of us who wish to reverse this trend toward socialism, beat the insatiably power-hungry monster back into a small cage, shrink the size and reach and interference and dominance of government in favor of individual, personal rights, opportunities and responsibilities.

The war is in progress, in Congress, in the media, in our streets, in New Jersey, in the little room in the back of the salon where the desperate housewives risk all for the perfect bikini wax.

Balance The Budget? Mission Accomplished 4-20-09

BUYING BULK OFFICE SUPPLIES
AND OTHER STROKES OF GENIUS.

By Dan Kennedy

Business & Media Institute

4/29/2009 12:14:28 PM

APRIL 20 WAS CERTAINLY A red letter day for America.

That was when President Obama held his first photo-op cabinet meeting, noisily giving them their marching orders: find ways to save $100-million in 100 days. And then he proudly told all of us that the head of Homeland Security, Janet Napolitano, had discovered opportunity for substantial savings in her department by *buying office supplies in bulk*.

I double-checked; I had not accidentally tuned into the Obama impersonator on Saturday Night Live. This was the real President, live, carried on several cable networks. I was watching Fox Business. And I'm sure everyone in its audience was feverishly scribbling notes and hastily calling their own high-level meetings to discuss this amazing revelation.

Forget the fact that, at this point, having spent trillions faster the average teenager can Twitter the latest breaking news about Miley Cyrus, saving $100-million is roughly equal to you or I figuring out how to save ten bucks this month. Forget the fact that while Janet has been devoting her attention to this bit of rocket science, her home state of Arizona is overrun with cross-border crime, kidnappings and violence, and, apparently our homeland security is being mortally threatened by all those returning veterans who *might* be right-wing extremists, so she *might* have bigger fish to fry. Forget whatever worries you might have about your job or business or retirement savings. All is well now that we've discovered the miracle of buying office supplies in bulk.

I defy anyone who claims the media is not in the tank for Obama, desperately protecting Obama, trying with all its might to mask this President's painful, shocking stupidity, to answer me this: had President Bush convened the cameras to tell the nation of this same discovery, how would the news media and the late-night comics have treated him? Had Governor Palin made this suggestion for demonstrating new commitment to fiscal responsibility in Washington, how would she have been treated?

The nights of the 20th and the 21st, I tuned into Leno's monologues and Letterman's Top Ten's. No mention of the Obama-Napolitano Economic Recovery Plan involving purchasing the big value packs of paperclips instead of buying them one at a time. I couldn't catch CNN or MSNBC mocking it every 3 minutes for days either, as they did Sarah Palin's "I can see Russia from here." For that matter, had Chavez pressed a book about the 5,001 ways America is evil into President Bush's hand,

and Bush later commented that it was "a nice gesture," how do you think that would have been reported?

It's really unfortunate that Napolitano's earth-shaking discovery occurred after the G-20 Summit instead of before – imagine the awe of all the foreign leaders had our president been able to bring this piece of news to them? World peace through nuclear disarmament *and* global economic recovery by buying bulk office supplies? He is a god!

Since Letterman missed it, here are the cabinet's other top 9 ideas for reducing government expense and waste, to offset the president's multi-trillion dollar spending spree:

#9: Michelle starts shopping at Costco, and discovers a second reason to be proud of America. Who knew you could get 5-gallon drums of peanut butter at such a low price?

#8: Replace the executives at Fannie Mae, Freddie Mac, AIG, GM and the UAW with captured Somali pirates. It's a two-fer.

#7: Time-share Bo the dog.

#6: Tax amnesty for Obama administration bureaucrats.

#5: Keep Texas but force Michigan to secede from the union. Maybe Canada will take it. Then we can say mission accomplished about national health care too. Sort of.

#4: Change Homeland Security to Homeland Shopping, and have Janet teach every American how to wisely use that extra $8 or $13 the president has put into their paychecks. She can go on Oprah once a week like Dr. Phil used to, then get her own show

– and the government can get the syndication money. We'll all be rich, then we can tax the hell out of ourselves.

#3: Buy poisoned food and toxic dry wall from China in bulk.

#2: Buy tele-prompters in bulk. We need them *everywhere* he might speak.

#1: Hey, if we're creating all these shovel ready jobs, shouldn't we be buying shovels in bulk too?

Can You Tell The Comedy From The News?

WHO'S FUNNIER: THE PRESIDENT OR HIS STRAIGHT MEN IN THE MEDIA?

By Dan Kennedy

Business & Media Institute

5/27/2009 10:34:42 AM

I AM HAVING AN EVERMORE difficult time deciding if President Obama is a comedian pulling our collective leg, or he really has as much arrogant disdain for the people paying all the bills he's printing as his silly statements suggest.

The most recent funny episode I've chronicled came on May 21 when, in one of his gazillion speeches a day, the president was sharply critical of past Bush Administration policies he characterized as based on ends-justify-the-means logic. I burst out laughing, and was surprised none of the pundits I saw discussing it afterward were amused. This guy *is* Mr. Ends Justify the Means. And he should be wearing a T-shirt that reads: "Irony Are Us."

Let's see ... he has merrily taken control of privately held companies, dictated to and disenfranchised shareholders and bondholders, ignored rule of law, threatened and bullied and arguably even endangered the safety of corporate CEOs, and blithely created more debt than all other administrations before him combined. He and his minions justify every outrageous act with the same argument: the urgency of the desperate circumstances we face and the long-term, future benefits of the radical New Society we are creating justify the means employed, however bizarre, un-American, non-transparent and secretive and hurried they may be. Then, with a straight face, he rails against end-justifies-the-means thinking. Remarkable.

Now as famous as Dan Quayle's spelling gaffe with the fruit of Idaho, Governor Palin is relentlessly pursued by her mention that she can see Russia from her state (she *never* said "from my house.") Is it really possible that Obama *can't* see the end-justifies-the-means dogma spread wall to wall and knee deep inside his own house? Is he a silly man? Or is this his real national, universal health care plan? After all, laughter is the best medicine.

But on that same day cable TV provided something even more hilarious than even the President might conjure. On MSNBC's "Morning Joe" they discussed the cover of the next TIME Magazine, devoted to, "The

Meaning of Michelle." The justification for yet another magazine cover given over to Michelle Obama? (After all, it seems the only magazine she hasn't been used on is Guns & Ammo.) Well, Michelle is of *unprecedented* significance and importance, according to TIME's spokesperson. His evidence – proffered admiringly, gushingly – was that "when Michelle wears a dress from J. Crew or a sweater from Talbot's, people run out and buy them."

Yes, honest, that's nearly a verbatim quote; he really did say this. Proof of Michelle's enormous, never before witnessed importance as a First Lady is her ability to move merchandise off retailers' shelves. Like Joan Rivers selling jewelry on QVC. But.

This has, in fact, been seen on an even grander scale not all that long ago, with another woman of the White House. I recall that the day after Monica Lewinsky was interviewed by Barbara Walters, department store cosmetic counters nationwide faced a stampede of customers demanding the brand and color of the lipstick Monica displayed on that show, its sales skyrocketed, and stores were sold out that same day. Unprecedented indeed.

If we let the president and the press continue committing such comedy, we may put all the professional satirists and comedians out of work, and I don't think Maher, Stewart, Colbert, the SNL cast, Leno and Letterman are going to be very happy donning those jump-suits and hard hats to work on all those shovel ready projects we keep hearing about.

You Will Wear White, and You Will Like It

OUR EMERGING DICTATORSHIP OF CLOWNS.

By Dan Kennedy

Business & Media Institute

6/3/2009 10:37:03 AM

IF WE WOULD JUST INFLATE our tires and get regular tune-ups, drilling for oil would be unnecessary.

Now one of the many czars of the Oz-bama Regime has blithely suggested we should all be ordered to paint the roofs of our houses white – that doing so would equal taking every car on the planet off the roads for eleven years. I wonder if whatever he's smoking is negatively affecting climate change.

But why stop there? If white roofs are such an energy conservation miracle, surely making all cars white would help a lot too, and since we are soon to have only Oz-bama Motors achieving the impossible 35-miles-per-gallon average, it'll be easy to issue the little eggs with wheels in one color.

And what about clothes? We can't very well have people wandering around outdoors on hot days in little black cocktail dresses or Baywatch-red swimsuits. If we let that continue, the icebergs'll melt and we'll all be under water. Let's mandate white for all clothes worn outdoors and restrict the wearing of colors indoors. For good measure, let's replace those big, black robes the Supreme Court justices wear with light white linen. In fact, maybe it'd be a good idea to eliminate the apparel industry altogether and issue everybody a white uniform.

It's been known for some time that cows' flatulence worsens global warming, so it'd seem prudent to outlaw beef, and, for that matter, outlaw any foods that give humans gas. Or at bare minimum, levy a huge tax surcharge on beef and flatulence-causing foods to discourage their consumption. He has decided to punitively tax sugar laden foods. Might as well tax every food that's bad for us.

Don't laugh. It's pretty hard to tell my goofy suggestions from theirs.

His administration resembles one of those little clown cars at the circus – it's amazing that there are so many clowns in there! They just keep coming out, one after the other. It's funny at the circus. It's not so funny when the clowns are confiscating companies, taking over entire industries, subverting established law, spending more money faster than any previous administration, and dreaming up mandate upon mandate. It's not so funny when you consider their obvious intent to dictate to us in every single aspect of our lives. Not so funny.

On Fox News Sunday, Mitt Romney put it succinctly: "The President believes an all powerful, growing government is the solution." Key word: all-powerful. Reminded me of President Ford's caution, that a government big and powerful enough to give you everything you want is big and powerful enough to take everything you have. Even your choices in color of paint or clothes, car you drive, food you eat, amount of money you are permitted to make or pay your employees.

Of course, no one cares much about the neighbor's ox getting gored.

But it's the responsibility of the media to take note of it, to challenge it, to sound the alarms and shine the spotlight on abuses of power. Not much of that going on. In their defense, they're busy, reporting on "Jon and Kate + 8," on Barack and Michelle's date night in the Big Apple, and on the little fruit-loop dictator in North Korea.

Personally, I think our budding dictator is a greater threat than any dictator elsewhere.

The $114 Billion Rusty Lawn Mower; the Dog That Didnmt Bark

OBAMA'S INVESTED OUR MONEY IN ANOTHER DEAD COMPANY.

By Dan Kennedy
Business & Media Institute
6/10/2009 10:13:43 AM

GENERAL MOTORS IS WORTH APPROXIMATELY minus $90 billion. That's a negative net worth of $90 billion. Into which the president has put about $60-billion total, for 60 percent ownership on our behalf. We have traded plus-$60-billion for minus $54-billion, a net loss of $114-billion. We as investors are upside down by even more than the bankrupt carcass we've invested in is upside down.

To do this magical deal, Obama had to commit massive financial fraud (by lying to us and GM stockholders about the company's certain bankruptcy while engineering it), trash federal bankruptcy law, conspire to steal bondholders' property and rights (making it insane for anyone to invest in any corporate bonds), create ownership nearly for free for the UAW, and extort the nation of Canada. He did this all in the name of saving jobs – while the result is, in fact, massive job losses, closure of thousands of small businesses (car dealerships) and by domino effect, thousands more. Well, Obama never claimed to be a capitalist, now, did he?

The little gas lawn mower sitting in your garage that might bring $25 at a garage sale is worth $114,000,000,025 more than our stake in GM. You should incorporate it as Brokedown Lawn Mowers Inc., call up Obama, and sell him half of it for about $180-billion.

For GM to break even and not need more money from us yet this year, it must sell 10-million cars between now and Christmas. This is about as likely as Obama going a week without making a "major speech" or the V.P. going a week without revealing some inconvenient truth. Fact is, they won't sell half that many. You mowing lawns with your little lawn mower would repay more of the $180-billion handed you than GM will be able to repay of the money we've dumped into it. And if you used $10 of the money given you to invest in a snow shovel, you'd be twice as viable as GM.

The president tells us GM will be in and out of bankruptcy in 2 months, 3 at the most. Another lie. GM is bankrupt and always will be bankrupt. Yes, a so-called new GM will exit bankruptcy court. But it will remain bankrupt nonetheless.

If it were just GM, we could chalk it up to amateur mistake-making and necessary learning on the job, and in the grand scheme, what's a few hundred billion dollars anyway? But the man with the messiah complex is engaging in comparably delusional, dumb and dangerous behavior on every front at a speed never before seen in the world. Our collective national bankruptcy is inevitable. Better learn to speak Chinese.

If there are any honest men or women in the mostly in-the-tank for Obama media, they should fess up that were this a Republican President taking over defunct companies, pouring in billions, steamrolling equity holders, appointing powerful czars left and right to run confiscated corporations and even entire industries absent Congressional oversight, they would be screaming for his head on a stick. The media's tortured-logic excuse-making for their dictator run amok is embarrassing. To his credit, Jon Stewart asked if the government might take over a profitable company or two. He mocked the government GM and AIG takeovers, but couldn't bring himself to actually say "Obama." Just "the government." As if the body of the snake was somehow freelance killing, without knowledge of its head.

Obama reminds me of an old, bad, crude, off-color joke I'll sanitize here as best I can: Guy comes into a bar with a big dog. Bartender says "You can't bring a dog in here." Guy quickly explains his is a uniquely talented dog – in fact, it can be handed 50 cents wrapped in a napkin and sent to the store to buy and bring back a pack of cigarettes. (I told you –

old joke.) Guy demonstrates. Dog runs out, money clenched in his teeth, is back at lightning speed with the cigarettes. The amazed bartender asks if he can do it too. Doesn't get the exact change, just hands the dog a $5.00 bill. Off goes the dog. Twenty minutes later, no dog. Forty minutes, no dog. They find him out in the alley, excitedly engaging in doggie love-making with a fluffy little poodle, the $5 bill under one of her front paws. "Sorry," the big dog says, "but I never had five bucks before."

He, suddenly rich with our money and credit, and drunk with power beyond anything he ever imagined, isn't coming back with anything for us anytime soon.

We've handed the keys to the liquor cabinet and Dad's sports car to a teen-ager and said "Please drink responsibly. And don't drink and drive." Nothing but carnage to come.

President OOPS-Bama

THE UNRAVELLING OF THE AMAZING OZBAMA...

By Dan Kennedy
Business & Media Institute
7/15/2009 2:02:10 PM

REJOICE! THE AMAZING OZBAMA IS slowly disintegrating into OOPS-Bama.

A couple weeks ago, I wrote about quietly growing, simmering buyers' remorse - the realization that the President is anything but his promise, that his change is far more sweeping and radical than most Americans imagined. Ever so slowly, but steadily, people are becoming disenchanted if not outright terrified or enraged. The latest to say "Oops!" is none other than Colin Powell.

By way of disclosure, I know Colin Powell personally, appeared with him on numerous public events over a span of several years, support the objectives of his charity (America's Promise), appreciate his service to the country, respect him and like him. But I was greatly disappointed (although not very surprised) by his abandonment of the Republican party and of John McCain in order to endorse Obama.

I say not surprised because, at risk of being misunderstood, I imagined in advance of his decision that the prospect of the first black American president would be irresistible, as the prospect of a President Kennedy was to my father and many other Irish Catholics in 1960. (Of course, JFK was a tax-cutting fiscal conservative so supporting him made some sense for other reasons.). If Powell admitted supporting Obama on that basis, it would be perfectly understandable.

Of course, Powell did not admit such a thing. Rather, he asserted that Obama offered needed changes in economic, social and international directions. He is now singing a very different tune.

Recently, from Powell: "...one of the cautions that must be given the president is that you can't have so many things on the table that we can't pay for it all. I never would have believed we would have budgets rising into the multi-trillions of dollars." In his speech way back at the 1996 Republican convention, Powell complained about the size and intrusiveness of government and cautioned that we couldn't afford more entitlements requiring higher taxes. In the recent interview on CNN, he echoed the same thoughts, advocating the smallest tax burden possible, and warning that Obama "has to start taking a very, very hard look at what the cost of all this is."

Amen, friend. Of course, since you encouraged voters to buy this czar-making drunken sailor with a messiah complex, you do bear some of the responsibility. Apology accepted. But please keep pressing the issue – and find a fiscally sane Republican you can support.

This, of course, has not been made nearly as much of by the media as was Powell's original endorsement of Obama. I recall the pundits on MSNBC, for example, gloating over that endorsement and endlessly repeating Powell's comments day after day then. I haven't noticed equivalent glee or exposure of his buyer's remorse now. Gee.

Recent Rasmussen polls show that, on the economy, on taxes, and on international affairs and homeland defense, a growing number of Americans expressing greater trust in Republicans than in Democrats. It's a bigger, broader manifestation of buyers' remorse.

And now OOPS-Bama is handing his Democrats a big, fat, ugly hot potato. He's making a power-grab for the entire health care system, a demanding that it be done with reckless haste, at epic cost during a time of unimaginable national debt, with unclear and indefinable benefit, and specter of evil unintended consequences even the blind can see.

The July 8th USA TODAY reported the failure of security at federal buildings – including the one housing the Department of Homeland Security. Journalists easily taking in bomb-making paraphernalia, assembling it once inside and strolled the hallways, undetected. Ten attempts, score 10 for the bombers, 0 for the government's security. Do we seriously expect folks who can't protect themselves and their own buildings to protect our health? Will they protect our right to unfettered health care choices, the quality of our health care?

These people didn't notice the Madoff scam growing under their regulatory noses for a decade. They encouraged Fannie Mae and Freddie Mac to – as Barney Frank put it – "gamble" with loosey-goosey lending criteria. They've managed Social Security and Medicare into impending bankruptcy. They can't or won't account for billions of dollars – lost abroad, in Iraq and elsewhere, and spent at home, in TARP. *These people can't manage the entry to a building.* Should they be managing the entire health care system? More will wake up. Unlike the dinner specials at Denny's, you can have substitutes here.

Like giant trees grow from tiny acorns, veritable revolution grows from small, smoldering buyers' remorse. Colin Powell is the latest canary emerging from the coal mine where the remorse is smoldering. The revolution? It just may look a lot like the Reagan Revolution. If conservatives can get their act together, America is getting ready to welcome their leadership.

It Has Come To This

GET EVERYTHING. PAY NOTHING. THE SIGN OF OUR TIMES.

By Dan Kennedy

Business & Media Institute

9/23/2009 10:32:41 AM

I'M IN THE ADVERTISING BUSINESS, so it's not all that easy to show me a sales pitch I'm shamed by. But I found one over the weekend while I was wandering around in a middle-class shopping mall in Jacksonville, Florida. In front of a store, a huge sign stopped my wife and I in our tracks. I said: «It has come to this.» The sign made this offer:

Get Everything. Pay Nothing.

Seeing that sign depressed me. Seeing lots of other people see it and fail to recoil in horror or at least burst out laughing depressed me even more. It's just like when I get depressed seeing lots of people watching and listening to the president on TV and not recoiling in horror or at least bursting out laughing.

Because that sign might just as easily be posted on the White House lawn.

People need to very quickly decide, en-masse, that this is, (to borrow from the rude but accurate Congressman who blurted the blurt heard 'round the world) a lie, and anyone peddling it, a liar. The current administration has put Truth in the number one position on the endangered species list.

The end game of the obscenely mis-named health care reform followed by the 2010 mid-term elections will reveal, bluntly, just how stupid how many of our citizens are. A public intelligence test is in progress. Is the public dumb enough to let its elected representatives buy, on their behalf, the Get Everything-Pay Nothing package or are most people smarter than 5th graders? Is the public willing to trade away their entire country for promises no one capable of counting could believe might be kept, or will it rise up in an ever-growing, evermore vocal resistance movement? Can Truth be saved from extinction?

Recently, President Obama suggested that government (ie. taxpayers) should provide "cradle to career" education for everybody. This is as good an example as any of the many Get-Everything-Pay-Nothing piles of steaming, stinking dung he is trying to peddle as perfume. The less radical, more conservative Rev. Jesse Jackson stopped short of that, instead merely proposing all college students have access to government loans at 1% interest – the same interest rate banks borrow at, he noted. Never mind that banks are strictly regulated by government to provide strong likelihood of repayments while college students are not such reliable credit risks. Or that it might build character to save up some money and work to earn money to pay for one's college education or at least some portion of it. Forget all that. Just take note of the fact that even the Reverend Jackson is not as far-left-leaning as Obama. No one is. Certainly no American President has ever been.

Senator Baucus, the Democrat hung out to dry by his President and his Party, became too toxic to stand next to overnight by daring to suggest that somehow, somebody might actually have to pay for the costs of gifting health care to all. Had he come to the microphone wearing a sandwich-board sign reading "Get Everything. Pay Nothing." he would have been much more warmly received.

If this is what we have come to, that a sales pitch so blatantly, outrageously, obviously a lie is eagerly bought, I fear for America and am embarrassed for us.

Al Gore's Hand in Your Pocket

GOVERNMENT GAMBLES WITH TAXPAYER MONEY IT DOESN'T HAVE ON A CAR THAT MAY NEVER SELL.

By Dan Kennedy

Business & Media Institute

9/30/2009 4:44:37 PM

GEE, WASN'T IT OBAMA WHO swore to end the influence of lobbyists in government?

So we should believe that Al Gore is not a big, fat lobbyist. It is pure coincidence that the start-up electric car company Gore is invested in and backing got a $529-million U.S. government "loan" to further development of its intended super fuel-efficient hybrid cars.

The first of those cars, humorously called the Karma, will sell for about $90,000. Later the company *hopes* – Obama's favorite strategy – that it will be able to build a more affordable $40,000 version, but there aren't even any plans on the drawing board for it yet. It's just a thought. Oh, and a bunch of the work on the car is occurring in Finland. As far as I know, Finland has not loaned them $529-million. Perhaps that's why it's so tough to find those jobs Obama's stimulus saved or created – they're in Finland.

This company, Fisker Automotive, not only has Jolly Green Giant Gore as investor, backer and advocate (ie. lobbyist), its other top investors include major "bundlers" of millions of dollars of campaign donations for Obama. Coincidence abounds.

The car is a pipe dream. If it had legitimate marketplace potential, there'd be no need to gamble on it with taxpayer money. Gore and his buddies are awash in ultra-rich fat-cat investors – their private jets are parked right next to each other.

Do you really want your tax dollars used as gambling ante, so Gore and Friends take less risk, and government bureaucrats get to play venture capitalist? And seriously, an $89,000 hybrid sports car? The specious argument given by Henrik Fisker to *The Wall Street Journal* (9-25-09) is that a lot of technology starts out very pricey then becomes affordable over time with mass acceptance and volume, like big screen plasma TVs that once sold for $25,000. However, I don't think we taxpayers ponied up $500-million to invent the whopper TVs.

This isn't about investing, oops, *lending* to technology development anyway. This is risking taxpayer money on a start-up car company with a ridiculously high-priced product to be and no dealer network. At some point, this company will be trying to compete with Toyota, Honda, etc., as well as the wounded but still very present Ford, Chrysler and Government Motors, and in luxury sports cars, with the likes of Ferrari. The last time I looked around, by the way, there's already a highly efficient hybrid car being sold. It's called the Prius.

This is no more or less than theft of taxpayers' money to reward campaign contributors and political insiders. It's a reverse re-distribution of the wealth; money taken out of the paychecks of all those "working people" the Democrats are always blathering about fighting for. That money then goes into the pockets of made-rich-through-politics con artists like Gore and hustlers who raise money for Democrat candidates for this very reason: to have it returned to them a hundred-fold. Further, in this case, we are subsidizing a company with the stated goal of developing *luxury* cars no "working people" will ever be able to buy.

And need I point out, we don't have the $529-million we just loaned for this scam? We are broke. Beyond broke. In debt to China and future generations up to our eyeballs. We have to borrow this $529-million in order to loan it out. This is the asinine equivalent of a bankrupt U.S. bank making loans to real estate speculators starting up muskrat ranches. In New Zealand.

If there's honest, legitimate opportunity to develop this kind of car, shouldn't we be loaning the money to an established American car company in which we are already heavily invested and already gambling on – not an upstart *competitor?* Shouldn't we be racing to beat any new boys like Fisker to the market?

If there is Karma, for which this phony-baloney car is named, then everyone in government, Gore, and the other hustlers involved with this theft and others just like it will come back in their next life as frogs in the Mohave Desert. Born there on a record-breaking, scorchingly-hot day.

APPENDIX 2

Key Point Review Checklist

CHAPTER 1

CHAPTER 2

CHAPTER 6

CHAPTER 7

CHAPTER 8

CHAPTER 9

CHAPTER 10

CHAPTER 17

Seeking a sudden surge of attention? Consider a prank...

CHAPTER 18

CHAPTER 19

Beware self-indulgence

CHAPTER 20

Don't take comedy for granted

CHAPTER 21

BUY A SHARE OF THE FUTURE IN YOUR COMMUNITY

These certificates make great holiday, graduation and birthday gifts that can be personalized with the recipient's name. The cost of one S.H.A.R.E. or one square foot is $54.17. The personalized certificate is suitable for framing and will state the number of shares purchased and the amount of each share, as well as the recipient's name. The home that you participate in "building" will last for many years and will continue to grow in value.

Here is a sample SHARE certificate:

YES, I WOULD LIKE TO HELP!

I support the work that Habitat for Humanity does and I want to be part of the excitement! As a donor, I will receive periodic updates on your construction activities but, more importantly, I know my gift will help a family in our community realize the dream of homeownership. **I would like to SHARE in your efforts against substandard housing in my community!** *(Please print below)*

PLEASE SEND ME _____ SHARES at $54.17 EACH = $ $_____

In Honor Of: _____

Occasion: (Circle One)   HOLIDAY   BIRTHDAY   ANNIVERSARY

    OTHER: _____

Address of Recipient: _____

Gift From: _____ *Donor Address:* _____

Donor Email: _____

I AM ENCLOSING A CHECK FOR $ $_____ PAYABLE TO HABITAT FOR HUMANITY OR PLEASE CHARGE MY VISA OR MASTERCARD *(CIRCLE ONE)*

Card Number _____ Expiration Date: _____

Name as it appears on Credit Card _____ Charge Amount $ _____

Signature _____

Billing Address _____

Telephone # Day _____ Eve _____

PLEASE NOTE: Your contribution is tax-deductible to the fullest extent allowed by law.
Habitat for Humanity • P.O. Box 1443 • Newport News, VA 23601 • 757-596-5553
www.HelpHabitatforHumanity.org

- Two CDs Of The **EXCLUSIVE GOLD AUDIO INTERVIEWS**

  These are EXCLUSIVE interviews with <u>successful users of direct response advertising, leading experts and entrepreneurs in direct marketing, and famous business authors and speakers</u>. Use them to turn commuting hours into "POWER Thinking" hours.

* The New Member No B.S.® Income Explosion Guide & CD (Value = $29.97)

This resource is <u>especially designed for NEW MEMBERS</u> to show them HOW they can join the thousands of Established Members **creating exciting sales and PROFIT growth** in their Business, Practices, or Sales Careers & Greater SUCCESS in their Business lives.

Income Explosion FAST START Tele-Seminar with Dan Kennedy, Bill Glazer, and Lee Milteer (Value = $97.00)

Attend from the privacy and comfort of your home or office...hear a DYNAMIC discussion <u>of Key Advertising, Marketing, Promotion, Entrepreneurial & Phenomenon strategies</u>, PLUS answers to the most Frequently Asked Questions about these Strategies

* You'll also get these Exclusive "Members Only" Perks:

- **Special FREE Gold Member CALL-IN TIMES:** Several times a year, Dan & I schedule Gold-Member ONLY Call-In times
- **Gold Member RESTRICTED ACCESS WEBSITE:** Past issues of the *No B.S.® Marketing Letter*, articles, special news, etc.
- **Continually Updated MILLION DOLLAR RESOURCE DIRECTORY** with Contacts and Resources Dan & his clients use.

To activate your MOST INCREDIBLE FREE GIFT EVER you only pay a one-time charge of $19.95 (or $39.95 for Int'l subscribers) to cover postage (this is for everything). **After your 2-Month FREE test-drive, you will automatically continue at the <u>lowest</u> Gold Member price of $59.97 per month. Should you decide to cancel your membership, you can do so at any time by calling Glazer-Kennedy Insider's Circle™ at 410-825-8600 or faxing a cancellation note to 410-825-3301 (Monday through Friday 9am – 5pm). Remember, your credit card will NOT be charged the low monthly membership fee until the beginning of the 3rd month, which means you will receive 2 full issues to read, test, and profit from all of the powerful techniques and strategies you get from being an Insider's Circle Gold Member. And of course, it's impossible for you to lose, because if you don't absolutely LOVE everything you get, you can simply cancel your membership before the third month and never get billed a single penny for membership.**

EMAIL REQUIRED IN ORDER TO NOTIFY YOU ABOUT THE GLAZER-KENNEDY UNIVERSITY WEBINARS AND FAST START TELESEMINAR

Name _____ Business Name _____

Address _____

City _____ State _____ Zip _____ e-mail* _____

Phone _____ Fax _____

Credit Card Instructions to Cover $19.95 for Shipping & Handling:

_____Visa _____MasterCard _____ American Express _____ Discover

Credit Card Number _____ Exp. Date _____

Signature _____ Date _____

Providing this information constitutes your permission for Glazer-Kennedy Insider's Circle™ to contact you regarding related information via mail, e-mail, fax, and phone.

FAX BACK TO 410-825-3301
Or mail to: 401 Jefferson Ave, Towson, MD 21286